Entering Emerging Markets
Motorola's Blueprint for Going Global

Guenter Schoenborn

Entering Emerging Markets

Motorola's Blueprint for Going Global

Second Revised Edition

With 18 Figures

 Springer

Guenter Schoenborn
Feldstraße 17
65529 Waldems
Germany

Originally published by Motorola University Press, 1999

Cataloging-in-Publication Data
Library of Congress Control Number: 2006920776

ISBN-10   3-540-31745-7 Springer Berlin Heidelberg New York
ISBN-13   978-3-540-31745-6 Springer Berlin Heidelberg New York

Springer is a part of Springer Science+Business Media

springeronline.com

© Springer Berlin · Heidelberg 2006
Printed in Germany

Hardcover-Design: Erich Kirchner, Heidelberg

SPIN 11662006   43/3153-5 4 3 2 1 0 – Printed on acid-free paper

This book is dedicated to Robert W. Galvin,

a great entrepreneur and people leader

Foreword

At Motorola they have firsthand knowledge of what it takes to make a company a global leader. Today, the company maintains sales, service and manufacturing facilities throughout the world, conducts business on six continents and employs a large workforce worldwide. But like many US corporations, Motorola's early engagement in emerging markets was limited until political changes opened up new opportunities for growth. Since then, Motorola has endorsed a strategy to sell its products, systems and services in these emerging markets and to help new governments establish a telecommunications infrastructure in their countries.

Motorola has turned this strategy into a reality throughout Europe, Asia, Africa, the Middle East and Latin America but the course has not been easy. It has taken vision, teamwork, and most important, a plan. In this book, we outline Motorola's working model for emerging markets: a four-step process that is bold enough to support an aggressive market penetration, but realistic enough for any business to follow.

Since Motorola was founded in 1928, its main objective has been total customer satisfaction. But satisfying customers can be a real challenge in an emerging market. This book details the experiences of Motorola executives with hands-on experience, who learned that they had to understand the demands of their new customers and consider their cultural differences.

Given the scope of this book, I cannot think of a better person to pull it all together than Guenter Schoenborn, who was at the frontline of emerging markets in Central and Eastern Europe, the Middle East and Africa and was also actively engaged in global emerging market assignments. He offers an invaluable guide for setting up a business infrastructure in new markets and collected the best, most practical advice from his colleagues around the globe.

I'd like to thank all the people who helped with this ambitious book, which will prove to be an invaluable resource in the years to come.

A. William Wiggenhorn, President Emeritus of Motorola University
Vice Chairman, GEM (Global Edu-Tech Management Group) and
President Executive Development Associates Consulting Division

Globalization is a reality in our world. Fully realized for its potential in the 20th Century and now rapidly evolving in the 21st, a business leader needs to keep pace. The American Chamber of Commerce in Germany has always sought to aid US companies making transitions from the US to Germany, and from Germany to emerging markets, whether in former Eastern Germany, Eastern Europe, or as far as Eastern Asia.

Economic markets often don't recognize national borders. This book details Motorola's remarkable success in developing strong, lasting positions in emerging markets worldwide. Their techniques and strategies have become case studies for other companies attempting to engage international markets. This book in particular is an exceptional tool for people new to international business and experienced business leaders entering new markets.

I have known the author, both personally and professionally, for over 10 years. Guenter Schoenborn's skill as a leader is matched only by his innovation and forward-looking approach. His acute awareness of the complexity of a globalized world created his meteoric rise within the ranks of Motorola and the success of the company internationally.

The methods used to globalize a corporation may be varied and complicated, but this book provides a clear, understandable framework to create lasting success.

Fred B. Irwin, President, American Chamber of Commerce in Germany
Chief Operating Officer, Citigroup Global Markets,
Deutschland AG & Co. KgaA

Preface

Welcome to the exciting world of emerging markets. This book deals with the strategies and processes applied by Motorola throughout all phases of emerging market entry and the experiences collected by individuals and teams throughout the last 25 years.

Motorola University Press published the first edition of the book some time ago. It was merely designed as a training manual for internal use. Recent suggestions from readers and their appreciation have encouraged me to produce this second updated and expanded version for the external reader.

Motorola's emerging market activities cover a broad spectrum. To enumerate all strategies, processes and people involved would fill hundreds of pages. Therefore, please accept that the content concentrates on essential information. Since the only constant in life is change, the processes and programs described are subject to review and modification to ensure ongoing success in the emerging market entry. Also, some of the people interviewed are no longer in their positions or in the company. This is due to natural replacement, while others continue our work with their new ideas. All the people and programs mentioned, however, were indispensable for our success in the past two decades of emerging market entry.

The general statements expressed in some chapters reflect the author's opinion and are not necessarily identical with the Motorola position.

Unfortunately, dedication to the emerging markets is presently overshadowed by the war on terrorism. By demonstrating our unbroken commitment to these markets, we wish to convey the message that terrorism cannot prevent us from our efforts to create a better, more humane world.

This book primarily deals with Central and Eastern Europe, the Middle East and Africa as a coherent Motorola business region. It would not be valid and complete, however, without considering some of the core activities from the Asia/Pacific and Latin American/Caribbean regions. I have therefore invited a range of executives and professionals from these emerging markets to enrich this book with their experiences.

In the end we are all members of a big family. Most strategies, processes and experiences described are more or less common to all emerging markets because of global design, strategic intent or just as common business practices. Moreover, we all share an ongoing learning and know-how transfer. Instead of inserting this in a special chapter, it made sense to incorporate all relevant information into the natural content flow. These parts are based on local contributions and interviews, personal research and networking as well as my involvement in quite a few global emerging market assignments. Nevertheless everything reported is equally authentic and real.

Israel, as part of the Middle East region, is not covered in this book since Motorola's success story in this country would deserve its own book.

It is the objective to offer a practical guide to the reader. Emphasis is therefore put on a broad range of interviews with and contributions from executives and professionals of all levels, functions and regions. In most chapters, illustrations visualize the content. The checklists and the business plan at the end will lead the reader through the entire market entry processes and allow her or him to design a complete business strategy for own purposes.

This book is not intended to deal with the history, politics and economics of the regions. Such information is only included to enhance the understanding of the reader in ascertaining where emerging markets come from and what they are developing into. I have also refrained from including figures and statistics, as they tend to date quickly.

I wrestled at length about the proper use of position titles, something which quickly tends to become a political issue. Any other solution but using those titles valid at or related to the time of interview or contribution does not make sense. I am confident that any successors don't mind their title being returned to their predecessor for the specific purposes of the book. I have also preferred to use short versions of titles, since lengthy titles in the corporate terminology might confuse the reader. The following abbreviations may help territorial orientation:

EMEA:	Europe, Middle East and Africa
CEE:	Central and Eastern Europe
MEA:	Middle East and Africa
LAC:	Latin American / Caribbean Regions
AP:	Asia Pacific Region

The strategies and processes are the focal point in this book, not Motorola. Therefore, consider Motorola only as a workshop for ideas while other corporations are working with similar concepts under a different label.

Enjoy reading!

Guenter Schoenborn, January 2006

Acknowledgments

Thanks to:

Motorola, for giving me such a great opportunity.

Bill Wiggenhorn, former Senior Vice President and President of Motorola University, who encouraged and enabled me to write this book.

All my friends and former colleagues who contributed to its content through interviews and by being role models.

The local employees in our emerging markets who gave more to me than I gave to them.

My bosses who trusted and empowered me to seek and go in unusual directions.

Joanne Hughes and Kirsty Gutperl, teachers and translators, who typed this manuscript and were of most valuable assistance in the editing process.

Table of Contents

Chapter 1 - Regions in Transition

Mainstreams and Driving Forces

Like any region or country, emerging markets are in permanent transition. They are surrounded by mainstreams, which determined their past and present, while driving forces lead them into the future.

Complexity and Diversity. This is the third dimension. Countries vary greatly in terms of size and their cultural, social, economic and political status. Populations are composed of thousands of ethnic groups; the African continent alone consists of 3000 different ethnic groups communicating in 1000 languages.

It is difficult to sum up countries that currently classify as emerging markets or are seen as potential markets in the confines of this book. Regardless of which accounting methods are used the number is large. A best estimate is detailed below:

	Countries	Population (in millions)
Asia/Pacific region	26	2.870
Africa	53	670
Latin America/Caribbean	30	453
Central and Eastern Europe	20	408
The Middle East	12	139

(These figures will not change significantly in the future. As societies mature they will be replaced in these records by newcomers because of the rapid growth of world population).

The Legacy of the Past. Cultures, religions and the course of history have shaped individual and collective experiences and expectations. This has created specific behavior patterns, which permeate contemporary life and business.

Throughout many centuries colonization covered up to 85 percent of world territory. It deprived people of their dignity and broke the backs of traditional cultures. Many of the artificial borders drawn by the colonial powers are the source of recent civil wars, especially in Africa.

Latin America was dominated by large landowners and military dictatorships while leaders in Africa feathered their private nests to the detriment of developing their own countries. Russia was always ruled by a small upper class, ranging from the dominance of the early monasteries and the Orthodox Church in the Czar regimes all the way through to Communism. Feudal tyrants governed the Middle East. The two World Wars changed the political landscape in Europe. The hegemonic wars of the Chinese, Japanese and the Western Powers, plus the Cultural Revolution in China caused a long period of stagnation in Asia.

The Impetus of Freedom. The fight for freedom in Asia terminated the long lasting European dominance. In Latin America most military dictatorships were brought to their knees by both peaceful and violent revolutions, and in South Africa apartheid was abolished as a result of increasing external pressure and boycotting.

The most dramatic changes took place in Central and Eastern Europe though. Powerful movements led by charismatic leaders caused the systems of government to implode. This was a very emotional time in history. I remember the concert opening the 1990 Prague spring season. Rafael Kubilek conducted "My Country" by the Czech composer Smetana. Kubilek had left his home country some 40 years before. Although seriously ill, he returned to Prague to support the young people in their vigil in Wenceslas Square during the uprising. This filled him with new vigor and he conducted a brilliant orchestral performance. The fervent applause sounded like the liberation cry of the whole nation.

This event and many others, like the 25th anniversary of the freedom movement of the Solidarnosc Union in Poland, remind us that freedom is the highest intrinsic value of mankind.

Transformation at Diverse Speeds and Intensity. The euphoria over all these changes created a feeling of exhilaration, but turned out to be more like a long hike, reflecting the strenuous technical and mental process behind it.

- The Central European states were privileged in starting from a poll position thanks to their traditional association with Western Europe. Those Eastern European states not blessed with national resources were held back by their low economic potential. Russia sought middle ground between those elements of the old system, guaranteeing law and order, and an economic and political path tailored to its culture.

- The Middle East is a melting pot of many civilizations dominated by a high diversity of cultural, social, political and economic conditions and interests. This aggravates the peace process, a further liberalization of trade and the creation of democratic structures - all prerequisites for further integration into the world community.

- In South Africa the abolishment of apartheid was followed by a slow move towards an equal employment and affirmative action policy, white and black extremism and sharply rising crime. In Africa, as a whole, many countries are still suffering under new dictatorships with different labels, anarchy and civil war. An increasing number of young leaders are distancing themselves from the image of a lost continent. This move is accompanied by promising economic performance.

- In Latin America unstable growth can be seen in a fragile environment. The short boom and recession cycles aggravate a consistent regional development. Stringent reforms and a liberal trade policy support the emergence of stable democracies and new economies. This is accompanied by periods of social unrest.

- In large parts of Asia economic performance outruns social progress as the saying in this part of the world goes "The body runs ahead of the soul." Traditions, in turn, hinder the formation of modern democratic societies. A better control of growth, a stringent financial management and strengthening regional trade will contribute to a more balanced development.

New Alignments. As former political networks have gradually broken down, new alignments have been built up by a young generation of unbiased leaders. This applies to the membership of the Central European Nations in NATO and the European Union. In Africa, the Organization of African Unity (OAU) was recently substituted by the African Union (AU) which is pursuing the objective of an African economic union. A free trade zone between Europe and the Mediterranean belt states is planned for the year 2010. The Free Trade Area of the Americas (FTAA) will finally consist of 34 states and is expected to become effective by the year 2006. In the Asia-Pacific region, the Association of South East Asia Nations (ASEAN) was recently expanded to "Asia plus three" including Japan, China and South Korea and has firmed up a free trade area consisting of 10 states. This powerful organization is pursuing the ultimate goal of an Asian economic and monetary union. These new networks are complimented by a multitude of co-operations, alliances and joint ventures in many fields at national, regional and international level.

Transformation builds bridges between the past and the future. The regions and countries are in various stages of progression, which are linked with former experiences and peoples' future expectations. It will take some time before the legacy of the past can be shaken off in the course of the 21st century, yet the driving force of freedom, prosperity and integration into the world community will continue to grow stronger. The regions are preparing for the challenge of the future.

Chapter 2 - The 21st Century Has Entered the Door

Globalization as the Driving Force

In the 21st Century we will face dramatic changes in political, economic, social and technological fields, with globalization as the driving force. This will bring along challenges and threats as well as evolution and revolution. Individually and collectively we are caught in the middle of all these changes. Some will improve and others deteriorate our lives. The speed and complexity of the paradigm shiftings will also generate more business opportunities than ever before.

The Future Political Arena. There are early indicators that North and South Korea may develop a better relationship. Cuba will take a more open stance and become more closely associated with the region. In Latin America, democracy and economic growth will determine the path of most nations. In Africa, the last bastions of dictator regimes will fall and pave the way to more stable partnerships. A strongly unified Europe will embrace both East and West. It is hoped that a peace treaty between Israel and its neighbors may overcome stagnation in the Middle East. Post war countries like Afghanistan and Iraq will gradually move to stability and freedom but have to pay a high price.

Civil Wars and ethnic conflicts will replace classic wars, while terrorism and crime will continue to move alongside globalization. This will require new military doctrine. All this will strengthen the role of the United Nations.

In these political processes, delays, setbacks and new conflicts will be unavoidable. In 2004 we registered 42 violent conflicts and wars around the globe. The endeavor for freedom, however, will win the upper hand in the long term since the greatest driving power in the world stands behind them: the people themselves.

The Economic Battlefield. Globalization will change the distribution of economic power throughout the world. The classical autonomy of countries will weaken and become restricted to legislative ruling, regulatory policy and trade support. Since no country can survive alone, larger trade blocks will be formed which will also protect and promote regional interests. The financial markets will dictate economic performance. Transnational corporations will gain more influence due to their large technology bases, strategic capabilities and global networks. The more they are forced to compete, the quicker productivity will increase (even quicker than the increase in demand). This trend will lead to an increase in unemployment. As a consequence of these events, systems of social provision in the developed countries will no longer be sustainable, especially when one considers the ageing population. By the year 2050, 2.5 billion people will be over the age of 60 compared to 600 million now. And when the economic mainstreams bypass the developing countries, no wealth will be created, economic development will stagnate and business will not grow. This would have explosive consequences should it happen. Recent riots against globalization organized by movements such as Attac would support this potential scenario.

Demographics and Resources: A Ticking Bomb. In the 20th century world population increased from 1.6 to 6.0 billion. By the year 2050 it will have reached approximately 9.0 billion. 90% of population growth takes place in the least developed countries. For this reason the gap between rich and poor will continue to widen. This will trigger a new wave of mass migration, which will flood into the wealthy countries and urban areas. It is estimated that by 2030 over 50% of the people in Latin America and Asia will live in mega cities. This trend will lead to a fight for the survival of the fittest. These demographic changes will be accompanied by a dramatic shortage of natural resources, renewable materials, food and drinking water. Even now 815 million people around the world are starving. In the worst case scenario it is anticipated that climatic changes will destroy and eradicate entire fertile regions in the second half of the century, while other regions will be flooded. The flood catastrophes and human tragedies in South Asia and New Orleans have affected our hearts. They emphasize the need for a global effort to preserve our world for the generations to come.

A Quantum Leap in Technology. Fortunately enough, a range of technological breakthroughs improving the quality of life and resolving some of the burning issues will defuse some of the ticking bombs.

Nanotechnology will revolutionize entire industrial fields. New and genetically manipulated materials will enable a range of innovative applications while robots and self-monitoring machines will control factories, offices, households and traffic flow. Chips that can be carried in the human body will offer preventative medical care and ensure that computers can cure sickness when it occurs. This will naturally increase mobility.

Breakthroughs in the field of genetics will defeat incurable diseases and revolutionize agriculture and food production. New natural resources will be exploited such as the fertilization of deserts, drinking water from icebergs, harnessing energy from the sun and oceans and planet harvesting. Last but not least, global communications will make the world smaller and more transparent. And with manned stations on Mars and moon, a new era of space exploration will begin.

Globalization. This will be the major driving force of the 21st century, but it will split the world into two camps. The supporters view it as a vehicle for fostering free trade, wealth and human rights. It will link nations and people, increase understanding for cultural diversity and contribute to the establishment of a better world.

The opponents fear that globalization will increase the gap between rich and poor and create new forms of nationalism, protectionism and even radicalism. Global anonymity will replace local identity, our code of values will degenerate still further, and the price we will pay for global links will be too high.

Globalization, however, is not just an economic model; it describes the evolution of our modern society in the 21st century.

The Impact on Corporations. Globalization is unavoidable, if we don't reach out, it will strike us first. Nonetheless, we will not wake up one morning and be instantly "global." Rather, globalization is an arduous process involving years of evolution - maybe even phases of revolution.

The typical "career path" of an organization starts with a strong domestic focus, continues with the development of an export business, mutates into a multinational company with selected regional hubs, and finally reaches the peak as a global player. Not every corporation is willing or capable of joining this elite club. Depending on the strategic intent and economies of scale, companies must decide where it makes sense to proceed and at what level to stop.

For Western corporations, the critical success factors for globalization include:

- The capability of the organization and its leadership to internalize change.

- The trans-cultural competence that will lead to new concepts of product design, manufacturing, marketing, distribution and support.

- The understanding that enculturation (which encourages new employees from emerging markets to become familiar with Westerners and encourages Westerners to become sensitive to cultural diversity) is not a one-way street.

- Adjusting products to the market and not markets to the portfolio (it makes no sense to offer high-tier products in a low-tier country).

- The readiness to take risks and invest in regions with no immediate return (this is critical).

Can Emerging Markets Keep Pace? The term "emerging market" has become a buzzword in today's economic lexicon. Nonetheless, scientists, economists and business people define it differently and draw different conclusions from those definitions.

- Classical economists simply distinguish between the Northern and Southern Hemispheres, assigning the designated "emerging market" to those countries located in the southern half of the globe. However, because the border is no longer drawn between North and South, this now presents a poor generalization.

- A similarly misleading definition is based on global regions (ie. Africa, Latin America, Eastern Europe, Asia, etc.). This definition also has been rendered obsolete given that rich and poor, mature and developing countries appear across all these regions.

- The International Labor Office (ILO) defines emerging markets by a range of demographic and sociological data under the heading of "subsistence level," a more accurate but also rather complicated evaluation.

- The United Nations specifies the Human Development Index (HDI), a formula based on life expectancy, educational level and income growth.

- The United Nations has also created the Least Developed Countries Index (LDC) comprising of the 36 least developed countries around the globe and the Most Seriously Affected Countries List (MSAC's): the 28 countries most vulnerable to economic crises.

- Emerging markets have nothing in common with the New Economy except that they may happen to be the markets buying their products and services.

Corporations, on the other hand, usually apply their own criteria to markets, depending on their strategic intent. Thus, a simple and straightforward definition that captures the key strategic elements as well as a historical component is this: An emerging market is any region or country that is undergoing a transition of a historical dimension, hereby transforming it into a market-driven economy and, thus, generating major business opportunities.

Looking at the world through this definition, it turns out that about two-thirds of the existing regions and countries are emerging markets. They are our entrance-ticket to globalization. Therefore, it is of primary interest to Western corporations to forecast how all of the political, economic and social changes will affect these countries. Most countries are still too busy resolving their own problems and will not be able to reach the same speed on the highway into the 21st century as mature countries. However, these countries do have the advantage of being able to skip some decades in the development process. For example, in the telecommunications field many countries can simply bypass declining analog technology and adopt digital up front.

The question "Can emerging markets keep pace?" may as well be changed into "Can we ourselves keep pace with all the changes around us?"

The main hindering force in any organization is not technology but the human mindset. Many people fear the bright, cold light of globalization and prefer the warm candlelight of their home market. As long as we, as organizations, are dedicated to constant renewal and a lifelong learning process we will be able to overcome these mental barriers and convert them into an accelerating force in the emerging markets.

Emerging Markets Come and Go. When we review these transitions over time a pattern of medium and long term cycles become visible.

Political and economic forces dictate medium term cycles. As present emerging markets reach maturity and become saturated new ones spring up as a result of political change: Cuba, North Korea, Libya and Serbia, to name one country from each region.

The rise and fall of countries and regions form long-term cycles over centuries. Internal and external forces dictate these changes. They range, for example, from geo-strategic and hegemonic conquests in the upward cycle to decadence, oppression or natural disaster in the downward cycle. Typical examples are the Roman Empire from former times and recently Afghanistan and Iraq, cradles of early civilization.

Which Are the Present Emerging Markets? The answer is simple for Central and Eastern Europe: After the dramatic events of the late 80's and early 90's, the entire region has turned into one large emerging market. The vast majority of Africa also falls under this heading. In the Middle East there are more and less advanced markets with some of them as yet untapped. The Asia-Pacific region and the Latin America/Caribbean region are rather different. Markets tend to be generally more advanced. Quite a few already have a history. There are larger, more mature countries like China, India, Brazil and Mexico. Others are still in an early stage of development such as Vietnam.

Cellular Communications in a Global World

The following contribution by Adrian Nemcek (President, Motorola Networks) explains the basic communication needs in the emerging markets and the support of telecommunications companies to satisfy these needs. This subject is also a driving force of much of the book.

"Telecommunications is Motorola's core business and the highest priority in most emerging markets. This explains the significance and potential of the emerging markets for Motorola and vice versa, as well as the degree of involvement on both sides.

All communities of people have common basic needs, which include food, housing, water, transportation, energy and communications. Communications allow individuals and groups to perform social and business functions, which improve the quality of life and enhance the economic level of society. These needs and functions are common across most industrialized societies from the most to the least developed. The marked difference between them is the level of infrastructure that has been put in place to facilitate the development of their national society and economy.

All emerging countries share a common interest in improving the strength of their economies and improving the quality of life of their people as quickly as possible. The rapid advance of technology has provided a means to facilitate that end. Both basic services such as communications and industrial value can be created faster and at lower cost than ever before, giving the developing countries an opportunity to level the playing field and move much more quickly into the ranks of the developing nations. Motorola's inherent strength in creating technology solutions and new markets aligns exceptionally well with the needs of the emerging markets.

Seen historically, private communications were governed by government monopolies in the telecom market. These nominally provided fixed wireless services in a non-competitive environment. The services were fixed price, fixed functionality and mostly limited in terms of accessibility in relation to geography as well as in time to gain service. The cost model for wireless telephony was expensive by today's standards due to the cost of installing an extensively physical network, which had to go not just to the last mile, but also to the last inch of every premises and customer that was to be serviced. Public pay phones and village phones became common place in order to minimize the cost of infrastructure deployment and to provide communal access in a totally tethered world.

The advent of wireless telecommunications has changed all of that. Although initially wireless networks were licensed to the existing public wire-line telecommunication monopolies, the mass consumer appeal of personal devices allowed the regulators to create competition through multiple cellular service providers. This had the effect of not only lowering the cost of service through competition, but also made the service more affordable through the economies of volume created by growing industry demand for handset and supporting infrastructure. Personal communications became available instantaneously, everywhere and relatively inexpensive. What a boon for the developing economies!

No longer did governments in the emerging markets need to plan out costly 10-year modernization programs to encourage in-ground telecommunication systems. Now wireless communications could be put in place in months rather than years at a fraction of the cost. Quality of life of the people and the ability to facilitate economic growth could be enhanced virtually overnight. The result has been a large extension and diversification of cellular communications networks on a global basis. Developing countries in Asia, Eastern Europe, Middle East, Africa and Latin America could now provide services comparable to most developed nations. The stuff that created the most developed nations in the world could now be put in place in the emerging markets in years instead of decades.

Motorola saw the potential of communications technology early on and created an organization that, like our products, is boundary-less. From the origins of Motorola's two-way radio business, the then International Sales Divisions of Motorola evolved into the global organization we have today providing our products, networks and services in every part of the world. Multinational local organizations evolved staffed with sales, engineering, marketing, supply-chain and finance skills. Local industry and government relations developed, which allowed Motorola not just to be an American company doing business outside the United States, but a global corporation, which was a contributing factor to every country and region. As the emerging economies embraced the promise of cellular communications, the global Motorola organization developed along with the emerging market economies to serve their growing needs.

Early participation in the emerging market economies evolved from pure sales and service in the country to local manufacturing. This provided value to both the local economy and Motorola. Eventually, the creation of R&D centers in the emerging markets created new future value. Seen in the light of the present market the emphasis has been gradually shifting from manufacturing to rapid intellectual value creation in the form of software. In the complex nature of cellular networks, over half of our engineers globally are software engineers and this proportion is expected to grow as products evolve to more software content on common computing based hardware platforms. The ability to create product development centers in emerging markets has created greater long-term value and can be implemented on a very flexible basis. Also, having a very diverse engineering population has allowed unprecedented levels of local customer support, product localization and market cost equalization. It's been a win-win for the local economies and for Motorola. Programs with local universities and government research programs have further benefited all parties.

A considerable proportion of Motorola's worldwide networks have been installed in the emerging markets, China and India being the largest with multiple networks and customers. The rapid growth of cellular networks in emerging markets will continue for many years to come. While the established economies reach a high degree of market penetration with cellular communications, the emerging markets have an insatiable demand to provide these services to their largely unserved populations. The forward-looking statistics for future industry subscriber growth indicate that over the next 7 years approximately 80% of new cellular users will occur in the emerging markets.

The future technology evolution in cellular networks from pure voice services to data and information services plus voice will also have significant impact and benefit in the emerging markets. 2.5 and 3G digital service networks provide a viable access for global Internet services. One of our first GPRS networks in a Middle East country became the backbone for internet café services in that country as wireless Internet services were not readily available. The demand on that network was immediate and unprecedented. The future world of Internet and information services through the means of cellular networks promises to bring communications, information and content to people everywhere and anytime. The demand in the emerging markets will be strong as those economies again can use this technology to rapidly grow and serve their populations and local commerce.

Motorola's vision to be a true global partner in the emerging markets by providing cellular communications network solutions has been an outstanding success. The dramatic advances in wireless telecommunications technologies yet to come, coupled with the demand for them in the emerging markets will create a very bright future. Motorola networks will play a prominent role in them."

Figure 1 below presents a graphical summary of the factors that influence the marketplace that have been discussed in the first two chapters.

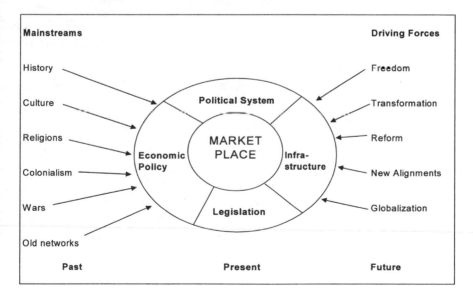

Figure 1: Mainstreams and Driving Forces

As the world becomes exposed to dramatic political, economic, social and technological changes in the decades to come, emerging markets will be more particularly affected. They have to cope with the backlog and future demand at the same time. It is a challenge for individuals and corporations to actively participate in this exciting process, which offers unique opportunities and experiences.

Chapter 3 - An Unprecedented Market Scenario

Like many US corporations, Motorola's early engagement in emerging markets was limited and cautious. It followed the political, social and economic development of the regions and countries. Special attention was paid to the elimination of barriers such as boycotts, business risks and ethical conflicts contradictory to our key beliefs and value systems. This policy resulted in various grades of commitment in different time periods. While Motorola's local presence in the Asia/Pacific region and parts of Latin America had been already established some decades before in the form of sustained investments, it maintained a low level of involvement in the Middle East and Africa for the above reasons. With the sudden opening of Central and Eastern Europe and the distancing from apartheid in South Africa the situation in these regions changed overnight.

The CEO endorsed a strategy to sell products, systems and services in these markets to help the new governments in the transformation process and to establish a telecommunications infrastructure that would improve the people's quality of life.

The Early Outpost Years

A Powerful People Message. In the late 70's our manufacturing operations in South Africa brought us face to face with apartheid. Motorola, like most investors, was in a dilemma: How could we exist and succeed in an environment that totally opposed our value system? Since the government policy was not predicted to change, local management decided to start the change from within. Gradually we introduced a participative work environment for the black workforce. People began to appreciate the power entrusted to them and the fairness and respect with which they were treated. The word spread around in the local community and among their families, still dominated by discrimination, a potentially explosive situation.

In 1985 Motorola decided to sell its South African holdings as a consequence of aggravating external circumstances. When the Human Resources Director left, he received a farewell card signed by every single black employee. This was one of the most powerful people messages Motorola ever received. It was the moment when we knew that we would come back.

A Region on the Move. No part of the world records such rapid change as the Asia Pacific region. It has left behind the structures of Western dominance, war and revolution, which my generation still remembers, and is growing into a new economic giant at the forefront of globalization.

With this in mind, Motorola started early and was one of the first American companies to establish local presence in Hong Kong in 1967. But unlike in Central and Eastern Europe where one macro-political event triggered market entry, we realized our goals in Asia in different time frames, at different speeds and intensity.

It required a sophisticated roll-out plan to balance the high market and human resources potential with the need for economies of scale. A mental barrier was the traditional Asian seller mentality, which aggravated the foundation of a buyer market for our products and services. This could only be achieved by a business philosophy and portfolio that positively distinguished ourselves from foreign and local competition and created added value. Another challenge was preventing our investments being eaten up by the large size and fast growth of the economies. The answer was to trust the self-propelling forces of localization.

With these strategies, Motorola laid an early foundation for its present high level of investment and commitment in the region. Moreover, a steadily increasing re-export of locally generated know-how, products and services is taking place.

Through Thick and Thin. John Steiner (Consultant at BGH, S.A. Argentina) recalls Motorola's start in Argentina. This is not only a contemporary document, but also an example of a close business relationship that survived many ups and downs.

"During the last months of the year 1959 BGH S.A., a successful Argentine corporation since 1913, obtained a special permit from the government for importing a few thousand CKD kits for local manufacture of black and white TV sets. BGH was previously involved with TV set manufacturing using inexpensive kits bought from local suppliers.

Import duties for shipment of parts to Argentina were rather high in those times and importation of finished consumer goods was banned. Import permits for kits were hard to get, but BGH managed to obtain one with one condition: A deadline had to be met, as the authorization expired on the last workday of 1958. It was November, there was less than 60 days left, and if the deadline was not met that single opportunity was to be lost.

It was then that BGH decided to get in touch with Motorola Overseas Corporation, the Motorola Company for Overseas distribution. The idea was to start manufacturing Motorola black and white TV sets in Argentina."

Dr. Julio Hojman, General Manager of BGH, who later on became its President, flew to Motorola's Augusta Boulevard Facilities in Chicago to meet the Galvins (the company owners) and several Motorola executives personally, all of them poised to develop new business ventures outside the USA. Within a few days Julio closed a deal with MOC. ensuring that Motorola did clearly perceive all the risks involved in such an unusual operation with so many unknowns. The Galvins decided to take the chance, maybe fascinated by the challenge of starting an entirely new operation, but also impressed by Julio's personal commitment to deal with the risks involved. After all, Argentina was hardly known in those times and, of course, nobody had ever heard of BGH. While it was difficult to meet the required schedules, and collection upon shipment sounded uncertain, the MOC Board still decided to trust Julio and give BGH enough credit to go ahead with the deal.

The Argentine Authorities closely controlled export transactions in this period, and they had to be executed under their own strict terms. Motorola did not have any previous experience in such deals; neither had they exported TV kits overseas before. To source and pack the required parts in time was a tedious and difficult job. After endless personal effort and overtime, the parts were finally shipped a few hours before expiry of the import permit. Needless to say, Julio and friends personally oversaw the shipment of all that material at midway point on route, just 12 hours after shipment from the factory. They had to hand carry packages and saw the boxes loaded on the plane in Chicago during a windy, white Christmas.

This was followed by Motorola alternators and in 1962 by two-way radios. 6 years later in 1968 Bob Galvin personally inaugurated BGH's two-way radio manufacturing plant in Tucuman City, 1000 miles North East of Buenos Aires. By 1976 production of two-way radios reached its peak. After 1978 import duties were dropped, product prices sank and technological changes snowballed. Traditional product lines were discontinued, only to be back again in 1989 with Motorola cellular phones.

It was mutual trust, confidence in the future and commitment to growth that always inspired both companies.

Through the Deep Valley of Reforms. Wilhelm Braxmaier (Director, CEE) was Motorola's first senior executive in Central and Eastern Europe before the iron curtain fell.

As a first step, Bill interviewed Motorola businesses about their expectations, readiness and willingness to commit. "The resonance was a mix of professional curiosity and reservation in leaving the comfort zone of a stable and structured, hard currency market and engaging in a risky and unstructured, weak currency market," Bill says. He faced two early challenges: He lacked a strategic fund because his colleagues were wary of sacrificing the operational budget; plus, he faced a stringent export control policy imposed by the US Government.

Bill's second task was to explore the new markets to assess their potential and limitations. "I found an infinite but not affordable demand coupled with an overbearing bureaucracy. With a few exceptions, like the police and the Red Cross, I had no direct access to my business partners. I had to work my way through the embassies as a first contact point to the foreign trade organizations, which were government controlled under the Ministries of Interior," he says.

Bill's findings also revealed a much lower industrial efficiency than he had expected. There was no added-value chain since research, product development, manufacturing and distribution worked insulated from each other. Customer orientation was nonexistent because in the seller market, demand always exceeded supply. The high proportion of military and defense production created huge problems for conversion to a civil product portfolio. Management did not carry any profit and loss responsibility, and collectivism killed any private self-initiative.

But there were also encouraging signs, such as enormous resources in basic research, a high educational standard and an overwhelming readiness to learn in anticipation of the major political and economic changes. Yet this in itself presented a dilemma. "One of my greatest challenges was to carefully reduce the over-expectations on both sides to a realistic level," Bill says, "Each reform process first generates an economic dip, and its steepness and length is the critical path determining failure or success. Countries and individuals may fall back to the old ways of thinking if the light at the end of the tunnel does not appear, while Western corporations tend to become impatient if there is no immediate return on investment."

Figure 2 below shows the differences between command and market economies with reference to development and reform.

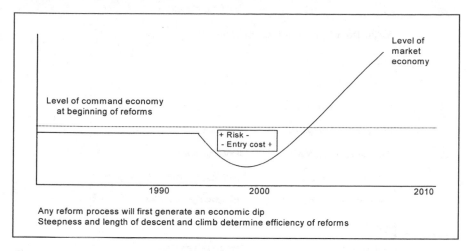

Figure 2: Economic Development vs. Reform Process

These experiences are shared by more or less all companies engaged in pre-mature stages of market entry. This early engagement offered several advantages. It demonstrated commitment under hardship conditions, opened the door to the country's structures and networks and laid a solid foundation for any future activities. The described processes are not unique. We see them again in countries like Afghanistan, Iraq, the successor states of former Yugoslavia and most certainly in any new emerging markets.

The list shown in Figure 3 shows the amount and complexity of transition from a command to a market economy.

Major Paradigm Shiftings in Emerging Markets	
From:	**To:**
Legacy of the past	Reach out for future
Stagnation of old systems	Dynamics of reforms
Former political networks	New alliances
Regional/country focus	Global integration
Adherence to old school	Readiness to learn and change
Command Structures	Liberalized environment
State monopolies	Privatized economy
Protective regulations	Deregulated markets
Arbitary legislation	Functional legislation
Selfish bureaucracy	Customer and service focus
State controlled policy	Liberal and competitive policy
Distribution of supplies	Buyer market
Unproductive operations	Profitable business
Plan fulfillment	Strategic intent
Reliance on system	Entrepreneurship
Employment by loyalty	Performance management

Figure 3: Major Paradigm Shiftings in Emerging Markets

Throughout the early outpost years corporations are exposed to risks and uncertainty. To overcome these critical phases they need perseverance, commitment to their goals and trust in the local partners. Above all, people with pioneer skills are required who can facilitate the necessary breakthrough.

Market "Exceleration" by a Total Systems Approach

Coined in 1992 by a group of executives designing a workbook for exploring new geographical markets, the term market "exceleration" incorporates two concepts: excellence and speed. It implies an accelerated and effective market entry by assigning this task to a team of specialists from a company's individual businesses and corporate functions. In a concerted effort, the team is entrusted to gather and analyze all information relevant to that market; align that information with the core competencies of the company and prepare a strategic-planning recommendation that contains a vision, mission, objectives, resources, requirements and timelines.

The selection of team members was based on what capabilities they could provide that were critical to the team's success. They had to:

- Be knowledgeable about the company and its decision-making structure

- Be committed in terms of time and dedication

- Have some sort of stake in the country or region

- Have experience and expertise working on teams

- Be sensitive to local culture

- Possess credibility within the organization

(These points are presented in Figure 4, Market Exceleration Flow-chart.)

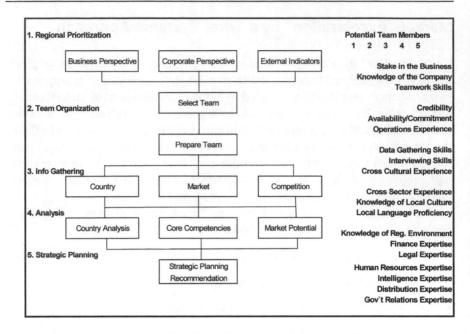

Figure 4: Market Exceleration Flowchart

The Need for a Plan. In fall 1999 we traveled to Austria. We were listening to Radio Hungary and we were amazed at how the democratic movement openly voiced its opinions although still under the weakening power of communism. We felt that something was in the air. There were many signals to support this although the sudden political change came as a surprise to Western governments and corporations. Most of them did not have a clue how to cope with this scenario, while political and economic science could not provide any empirical models. There was no plan.

The most prominent victim was the German government. Although the Germans on both sides of the wall had longed for their re-unification for 40 years, the government had no plan. Within a few weeks, a re-unification master plan had to be prepared. It was obvious that this plan could not avoid all pitfalls due to the time constraint placed on its preparation. CEO's soon recognized that the entry into the emerging countries could not be mastered by a "business as usual" approach but that it would require a concerted effort, a structural process and innovative ideas.

Applying the Team Approach to All Market Phases. We soon realized it would make sense to pursue this team concept not only when we were exploring an emerging market, but throughout later phases of the market-entry process. (These phases are covered in detail in subsequent chapters).

It became crucial to bundle our efforts and resources in view of prevailing hardships, such as the lack of local infrastructure, complicated logistics, remote management and a basket full of last minute surprises.

The team approach relied on ongoing mutual communication and coordination; a sustained process of mutual learning; and the sharing of know-how, resources and information. This enabled us to critically review our policies and procedures and make timely decisions. The Total Systems Approach is not new. Explorers and conquerors in ancient times were already accompanied by an army of specialists; engineers, architects, lawyers, geologists, priests, doctors and many others.

Art Condill (Country Manager, Saudi Arabia) summarizes his experience with the team approach:

"I was parachuted in, and there was no organization in place. I had to familiarize myself with the region in a crash course process, and I began to develop an organizational structure and distribution network from nothing. The team meetings offered me a tremendous shared learning and networking opportunity, they became a catalyst for our market entry, and without them we would not be where we are today."

Figure 5 shows the diversity of issues that affect an exploration startup.

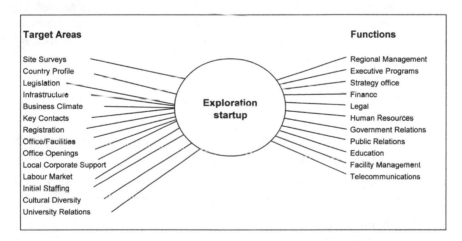

Figure 5: Emerging Markets - Total Systems Approach

Platforms for Steering Team Activities. The intensity of cooperation and team spirit, however, initially differed between Central and Eastern Europe, and the Middle East and Africa. While in Europe we worked together from day one and developed an esprit de corps, the case was different in the Middle East and Africa. When we took over responsibility for

these regions we found a confederation of independent Motorola companies that had already been doing business there for several years. Therefore, one of our first endeavors was to collect the various businesses, pool
them together and apply what we had learned in Central and Eastern
Europe. Within a reasonable period of time, we achieved the same cohesion because people recognized that together we worked faster and better.

To preserve and further develop this cooperation, we afforded ourselves
the luxury of institutionalizing a series of staff and team meetings. Although we had to fly in people from far away which was time and cost
consuming, the benefits of these communication forums were rated higher.
For many of our employees, who were spread over large territories in a
stand alone situation, this was the only occasion to get rid of these problems, share information with their colleagues, receive new inputs and return with a higher confidence level.

An interesting initiative was the facility meetings. Originally intended to
serve as a possibility to discuss facility and housekeeping issues with all
the tenants in the office building, they quickly became a roundtable for
discussing business with friendly companies.

The Four Phase Approach. When we looked at developing a model for
entering an emerging market, we divided the process into four phases. The
steps are bold enough to support an aggressive market penetration but
small enough to enable businesses to follow. The phases allow management to review the progress periodically and change direction if necessary.
The four phases are:

1. The exploration and pre-startup phase, a research-intensive phase that
   usually takes a year to complete.

2. The startup phase, roughly a two-year process marked by the
   establishment of a representative or branch office.

3. The consolidation phase, another approximately two-year phase that
   occurs when the business matures and becomes more stable.

4. The maintenance and expansion phase, which usually begins after
   five years in the country.

This model was deemed most appropriate for ensuring a smooth and efficient market entry that took into account:

- Major time frames.

- Different levels of progress achieved by the individual countries and our businesses.

- Varying requirements for people, resources and processes in each of these phases.

- Anticipation of change in the organizations and company.

A balanced allocation of investment and resources between the emerging markets and other markets of the company.

> *To be successful in the emerging markets corporations need a business plan, which can be implemented in the form of a total systems approach. They also need to decide on a structural process. This must be bold enough to allow an aggressive market penetrator but small enough for the organization to follow.*

Chapter 4 - The Exploration and Pre-Startup Phase

Laying the Foundations

A number of critical steps are involved in the first year of market entry, the exploration and pre-startup phase. These phases allow teams to research, set priorities and strategize in a way that will help build the foundation for the company's success in an emerging market. In this first phase, a company follows these process steps:

- Appoint a champion

- Determine positioning strategy

- Obtain top management commitment

- Establish selection criteria

- Prioritize countries

- Perform country exploration

- Develop strategic recommendations

- The beachhead concept

- A scenario planning case

- Run country awareness programs

Appointing a Champion. The complexity of the task at hand demanded that we appoint a champion who was a high-level, competent, dedicated and recognized executive. To do this, the CEO created the position of Regional Director, whose major responsibilities are governed by the strategic intent of the corporation. His or her duties include:

- Taking a lead in developing a vision, mission, strategies and objectives to make the company a prime supplier of equipment, systems, components and services in the region.

- Driving a coordinated process to meet and exceed the expectations of customers and partners while growing a profitable business.

- Creating a structure that supports a one-voice, one-face approach for our partners, and a climate that promotes team effort, enhances learning and generates added value.

The Regional Director is supported by champions of the corporate support functions including the strategy office, finance, human resources, legal, government relations, communications, intellectual property, facility management, telecommunications services and education.

Our human resources department helped ensure a channeled market entry. H.R.'s mission was to:

- Professionally and proactively advise and support the corporation and its sectors, groups and divisions in developing markets.

- Establish a culture that supports our key beliefs, goals and initiatives and makes the company a premier employer in the region.

- Develop, implement and practice consistent strategies, policies and procedures that blend the company's human resources charter with local labor practices.

Brian Bedford (Human Resources Director, EMEA) recalls that he and his colleagues were positively surprised that the changes happened so quickly. "We spontaneously appointed a Human Resources Director and fixed the organizational integration, budget and headcount afterwards," Brian says. The company's first pilot program in the region was a human resources task force to investigate the labor environment in some of the target countries and its application as a role model.

The Strategic Positioning Process. One of the primary considerations in the pre-startup phase was how the company should position itself in the emerging markets. Similar to other large corporations, Motorola is a complex organization divided into sectors, groups, divisions and numerous operations, all represented at country, regional and global levels and supported by a range of corporate functions, also organized by function and geography.

"We company executives had the opportunity to review this structure for its organizational effectiveness and customer focus. We needed to decide if the company should continue 'business as usual' and end up with individual Motorola businesses in each country or create an organization that would offer 'one-stop shopping'. In order to maximize our internal effectiveness, it became obvious that we should continue to use a decentralized approach", Parviz Mokhtari (Director, CEE / MEA) states. "One of the company's strengths is the autonomy of its sectors, groups and divisions in developing technology arenas and market segments. But at the same time, it was important to represent the company externally as unified to avoid confusing our customers. The result was an organizational pattern we called 'internally decentralized and externally unified'" (This pattern is displayed in Figure 6.)

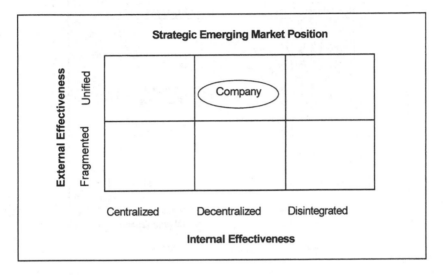

Figure 6: Strategic Emerging Market Position

We learned our lesson in the Czech Republic in 1991, when a group of Motorola executives visited the Ministry of Transportation and Telecommunications. The deputy minister, a very polite gentleman, displayed 17 Motorola business cards on a conference table and said: "Motorola is a very impressive corporation, and we would like to start business with you. But who is my contact point? I have cards from Chicago, Phoenix, London, Paris, Wiesbaden and so on. Let me give you some friendly advice: You cannot do business in this manner in our country."

This story was one of the decisive factors for our unified market entrance strategy. The unified approach offered some distinct advantages:

• Businesses were prevented from entering each country on their own.

• Dissipation and duplication of efforts was avoided.

• Business partners were not confused.

In line with this concept, the CEO initially approved the concept of shared offices and the positions of Country Manager and Business Development Manager.

Figure 7, illustrates the advantage of a structured process.

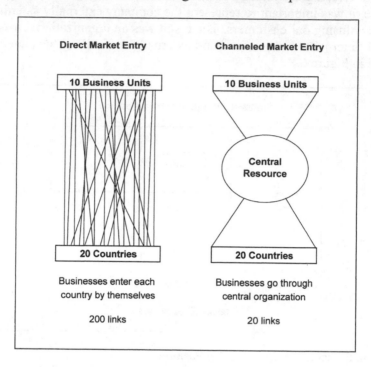

Direct Market Entry

10 Business Units

20 Countries

Businesses enter each
country by themselves

200 links

Channeled Market Entry

10 Business Units

Central
Resource

20 Countries

Businesses go through
central organization

20 links

Figure 7: Decentralized vs. Centralized Approach

The Shared Office Concept. The major benefits derived from this approach are obvious:

- Having only one office in each country fosters awareness and corporate identity, improves accessibility for persons from outside and limits confusion in the marketplace.

- The shared infrastructure, reception and secretarial services, office machines and equipment and telecommunications, increases efficiency and reduces operating costs.

- Centralized facility management maintains the office and releases the businesses from this administrative burden.

- People working in the office are able to share learning and know-how, which contributes to cohesion, team spirit and country focus.

- A sublease agreement between the corporate office and the businesses provides clear rules for office utilization and cost allocations. All users are treated fairly and equally.

As with most policies, there are a few exceptions. The nature of an operation may require a separate building and location, such as in the case of R&D centers, manufacturing plants or service and support shops. Large territories will probably require sub-offices in several of the large cities as well as in remote areas.

In 1990, I was traveling in Budapest and met by coincidence one of our general managers on the street. I asked him what he was doing there, and he told me that he was looking for an office. I alerted him that our company had made a decision to establish only one office per country, and this office would be shared by all businesses. He was skeptical and thought the setup would be expensive, inflexible and take months before he could move in. We went to dinner and I proposed a deal: He would wait only four weeks and by that time, we would have an office with an attractive space for his salespeople. After four weeks, he moved in and the arrangement was a success. This story illustrates the burden of turning around an organizational culture.

The following leadership models proved to be critical to our success throughout initial market entry.

The Country Manager is primarily assigned to a larger country with an established telecommunications infrastructure and where Motorola already has its own operations, agents and distributors. His or her responsibility is to link country opportunities and company capabilities in an ambassadorial role, and to streamline activities toward our vision. Major duties and responsibilities are to:

- Act as the company's key and legal representative in the country
- Be the interface and link between the country and the company
- Enhance corporate identity
- Balance country and business interests
- Assist businesses in becoming properly positioned in the country
- Promote business opportunities and key account management
- Represent the company's interests to government, national industry and trade associations

- Proactively pursue and comply with country legislation and protocol issues

- Improve the company's image and brand awareness with its key publics

- Create and lead an efficient and dedicated country team

- Manage the office and coordinate country operations

- Position the company as a good citizen, technical leader and premier employer

According to Richard Lada (Regional Director, CEE) the role of Country Manager is a broad one. "In its most simplified definition, it means adding value to Motorola in the country," Richard says. "This takes many forms: as an effective interface to the country's government and key publics; as a catalyst to get a business started in the country; by assisting a Motorola business already operating in the country in a critical situation; and by creating an environment of cooperation among Motorola businesses."

Another key focus of a Country Manager is to create a vision of how the company should look in ten years, and then pursue strategic initiatives to achieve the vision. "Hopefully over time, Motorola's stature, its perceived value by key publics, grows significantly. So the role of the Country Manager is a very creative one, and it's a challenge to know where the best place is to spend energy so as to have the most impact."

Yet, Richard concedes that the role of the Country Manager is not that well understood within the company. Another barrier is that the role has much responsibility but not much actual authority. So what remains critical to success is a Country Manager's ability to develop influence with businesses throughout the corporation. "Influence is something that gets created little by little over time when you have succeeded in adding value to partners - a Motorola business, an outside customer, a colleague," Richard says.

A company's name and reputation among customers, government and decision-makers is determined by its appearance as a homogeneous entity and by the performance of its individual businesses. "The results of our local company are measured by the success of each of the businesses as well as by the country profit and loss statement," says Thomas Szekeley (Country Manager, Hungary). "So one cannot survive without the others, and the Country Manager is in the middle, aligning the various interests and activities to the needs of the country and our customers."

The Business Development Manager usually works in a small or medium country with neither an existing telecommunications infrastructure nor a Motorola presence. The role is more product-based and oriented toward market exploration and development. The responsibilities of the business development manager include:

- Ensuring a smooth and efficient market entry by establishing contacts to key publics and properly positioning the company in the country

- Performing market research to assess the market structure, potential and mechanics

- Assisting our sectors, groups and divisions in developing the market segments for their systems, products and services

- Identifying and promoting strategic business opportunities with public and private customers

- Creating awareness for our brand by organizing participation in local events, such as exhibitions, and by driving image campaigns

- Providing guidance and support to our businesses in regulatory, frequency, spectrum and type approval issues

- Representing the company's interests at the country level and acting as the company's representative

- Managing the company office and enhancing corporate identity

Because the Country Manager and Business Development Manager roles are fluid, some elements of the job descriptions are identical. Depending on the country's strategy plan, a small country may start with a Country Manager while a major country may begin with a Business Development Manager. Normally, the first position is filled with a local citizen who knows the country inside and out, while a Motorola expatriate with local roots occupies the second position.

To help support employees in these demanding and complicated positions, the strategy office created a mentoring program. A Senior Executive is assigned to each Business Development Manager to act as a coach and counselor in the initial market entry phase.

Other Forms of Country Leadership. In some markets, it makes sense to deviate from the Country Manager or Business Development Manager template and start with a Branch Manager. This may be the case when a country's protocol, such as in the United Arab Emirates, could result in potential conflicts of interest with official sponsorships. In countries where the company has no strategic interest but, nevertheless, needs a small office, an Office Manager or a Senior Secretary acting in this function may be sufficient. Both positions are more administrative but may gain more responsibility as the company upgrades its local presence over time.

Top Management Commitment. Before moving forward, we had to obtain management buy-in to proceed with material investments in new markets. We needed to secure decisions from upper and lower levels in the organization. In the beginning, the system broke down occasionally. It happened, for instance, that a Regional Manager had committed to an office, but top management had other priorities. Similarly, top-down decisions were not understood or supported at the local level. Executives were as concerned about risking no return on their investment as they were about missed opportunities. Budget spending was another common concern, and some experts developed highly sophisticated excuses when it came time to commit to an office. To eliminate such decision-making problems, we implemented a clear decision matrix, and inconsistencies disappeared as our collective experience grew.

The Senior Executive Program (SEP). As a mighty catalyst, the Emerging Markets Senior Executive Program plays an important support role. Initiated in 1991 by the CEO it was composed of up to 25 vice presidents and officers across all corporate sectors and functions. The objectives of the program were as follows:

- Enter emerging markets: faster, better, together

- Take the processes and methodologies, and apply them to the world's other emerging markets

- Capture and codify organizational learning to change the company

The kick-off SEP meeting was held in Budapest in 1991 followed by periodic conferences in various emerging market cities. The talks are usually coupled with a major local event, such as an office opening. Also, ad hoc meetings to attack specific burning issues are conducted. Some of the major accomplishments of this team are:

- The first emerging markets entry "cookbook".

- Design and implementation of the business development manager concept

- A site visit process and mapping for social, political, technological and economic issues

- Latin America spin-off

- Joint meeting with Asia/Pacific Management Board

- Focus on key issues such as financing

- Close interface with the emerging market teams

The local people highly appreciate this institution because of the expertise, judgments, perspectives and decision power that comes out of the meetings. They allow participants to gain tremendous experience, share innovative ideas, "bond" with colleagues and make an impact on the corporation.

Establishing Selection Criteria. The world is full of excitement and untapped opportunities, which leads to a great temptation for companies to want to be everywhere at the same time. The German philosopher Emanuel Kant had expressed his longing for this sheer impossibility even in the 18th century: "Only he who has thought and understood the world as a whole will never perish again."

Some corporations fell victim to their desire to penetrate emerging markets and withdrew from the countries because they had neglected their due diligence homework, overestimated the return on investment and underestimated the high overhead costs of transportation, customs duties, import and export taxes, expatriate housing and more.

In early 1990, I was a member of a delegation of one of our businesses. We benchmarked an electronics and radio communications factory in Voronezh, 300 miles southwest of Moscow. They were converting from military to civil products and were desperately looking for a Western partner or buyer. The manufacturing equipment and processes were some decades behind Western standards. The management also showed us a huge, empty production hall they had built shortly before the conversion, which made it superfluous. They offered it to us for a token price on the condition that we take over the workforce. Unfortunately, the attractiveness of the offer paled in light of unmanageable, expensive logistics.

This case illustrates how difficult it can be to maintain a balance between opportunities and risks. The process requires strict selection and prioritizing in view of the complexity and diversity of emerging markets.

In order to determine which decisions are practical and of priority, it is customary to use "Selection Criteria for New Markets" demonstrated in Figure 8.

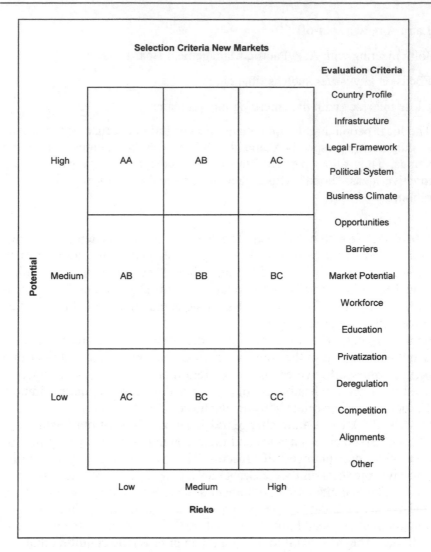

Figure 8: Selection Criteria New Markets

The A-B-C analysis helps to solidify our decisions and prioritize our investment. In the AA countries local pressure is a must, whilst it is wise to stay away from the CC countries. BB countries are ambivalent.

Scenario Option Development. Motorola primarily uses scenario option development: a structured process to analyze, systemize and evaluate complex situations and anticipated changes to choose and prioritize projects in emerging markets. Scenario option development supplements the classical, quantitative planning tools that are no longer sufficient to fore-cast major qualitative changes. Thus, strategic options and decisions can be built on more stable assumptions.

A typical scenario option development follows these steps:

1. Draw out the focal issue

2. Identify external factors and forces

3. Prioritize for impact and uncertainty

4. Construct the scenario framework

5. Check consistency with key factors

6. Create the scenarios

7. Review implications and early indicators

Scenario option development meetings are under the auspices of the Regional Director and the strategy office, and are attended by senior business and corporate representatives who possess an in-depth knowledge of the region. The programs are enriched by presentations from outside experts such as professors, government officials and consultants, while an experienced facilitator leads the process. The outcome is a regional grid reflecting on its axes the best and worst assumptions for the governing parameters. The countries in the region are then positioned within the grid, in terms of both present status and forecast migration.

A vital element of scenario option planning for telecommunication companies is the evaluation of telecommunications opportunities versus country risk factors. This pertains to infrastructures, equipment, systems and services within the framework of government policy. Multinational corporations' readiness to invest is closely connected to the status of liberalization, privatization, spectrum management, trading terms, legislation, security level and economic growth.

Country Prioritization is largely based on the results of scenario option development but also takes into account other determining factors. Field research may reveal additional positive or adverse conditions that are so pronounced that they influence the original decision in a different direction. For example, a fortunate discovery like that of vast oil and gas fields alters business strategy. By contrast, a planned investment into local manufacturing may be canceled when dangerous ground pollution is discovered. In addition, public indicators may call for a quick deviation from the original planning recommendation. These include political unrest, radical government change, rising extremism or major financial crises.

Country Exploration. During this intense research period, scrutinizing the prospective market from many perspectives is also important. We call this process country exploration.

The Desk Survey. In this phase, we identify information sources and try to get as much empirical data up front as possible. Data is available from sources such as:

- International and regional organizations (see listing in the Appendix)
- Western and local ministries of economics
- Foreign trade organizations
- Embassies and consulates
- Chambers of commerce
- Western law firms and their local affiliates
- Local universities
- Publication services
- Recruitment agencies
- Other multinational companies
- Company internal resources
- Internet and intranet

It is crucial to the success of the desk survey that the following points are observed:

- It is important to formulate questions in writing in as much detail as possible. A well-designed questionnaire has proven to be very helpful. Naturally, the output will be as precise or as vague as the questions are.
- A personal dialogue will increase your counterpart's understanding of your needs and his or her willingness to assist. If you cannot do this yourself, ask other professional functions to take this over for you.

Many useful questions can be found in the Appendix to this book.

The Field Survey. Like the desk survey, the field survey requires a timely and thorough preparation to make it effective. We consider the following rules essential for the mission:

- Prepare lists of people and institutions to call. Ask your local contacts to assist you in this process. Some of the best resources are the local accounting firms and law firms.

- Develop an agenda with detailed names, titles, addresses and functions of your ideal interviewees. Prepare and forward them a list of topics. Of course, it is crucial to spell names correctly and use proper titles.

- Once the agenda is set, plan the visit, obtain a visa and book flights and hotels. Canceling a visit because you misunderstood visa requirements and cycle times is embarrassing.

- Limit your daily schedule. If you plan more than four interviews, you risk running late and ruining the timing. Be flexible for last minute rescheduling requirements and have backup plans built into the agenda.

- As part of the travel plans, order a car with an English-speaking driver who is available to you throughout the program. While this is more expensive than using local taxis, it increases your personal safety, and ensures compliance with the agenda.

- Come to the meetings well prepared so you can use the available time and expertise of your partner most effectively. Inform yourself up front about local protocol to avoid mistakes.

The Information Analysis. The subsequent step to information gathering is analysis. In the analysis process, pay special attention to:

- Market selection, to achieve sufficient profit and return on investment

- Core competencies, to ensure that your company brings the best array of required competencies to a new market on a timely basis

One note of caution: don't rely too heavily on the empirical data. It is vital to avoid premature assumptions. The biggest error you can make is lacking confidence in the potential of a country and its people. Be open to new ideas and innovative ways. People can only prove their capabilities if they are given a chance, and in most cases, the empirical information and resulting conclusions are positively exceeded in reality.

The Overview Matrix. For compiling your findings and assumptions, you may find it helpful to use following matrix. The chart provides a condensed rating of those factors that are both supportive and non-supportive to the company's vision.

Subject	Supportive/ Non-supportive	Subject	Supportive/ Non-supportive
Country Profile	1 2 3 4 5	Labor Market	1 2 3 4 5
History and Culture	1 2 3 4 5	Employment Laws	1 2 3 4 5
Demographics	1 2 3 4 5	Forms of Local Pressure	1 2 3 4 5
Government Politics	1 2 3 4 5	Property Acquisition / Lease	1 2 3 4 5
Legal Framework	1 2 3 4 5	Local Content Requirements	1 2 3 4 5
Economic Indicators	1 2 3 4 5	Profit Expatriation	1 2 3 4 5
Trading Policy	1 2 3 4 5	Tax Structure	1 2 3 4 5
Business Opportunities	1 2 3 4 5	Traffic Tariffs	1 2 3 4 5
Business Barriers	1 2 3 4 5	Local Incentives	1 2 3 4 5
Market Potential	1 2 3 4 5	Import/Export Procedures	1 2 3 4 5
Infrastructure	1 2 3 4 5	Customs Procedures	1 2 3 4 5
Lifestyle	1 2 3 4 5	Licensing Requirements	1 2 3 4 5
Education Systems	1 2 3 4 5	Asset Protection	1 2 3 4 5
Workforce Quality	1 2 3 4 5	Intellectual Property Protection	1 2 3 4 5
Management Style	1 2 3 4 5	Security Level	1 2 3 4 5
Labor Relations	1 2 3 4 5		

Market Selection. The grid below allows you to identify and rank the markets and to rate your competitive advantage to customers, such as product portfolio, support and services, quality and cycle time, and cost. Perform this analysis for each sector, group or division. As a result of this analysis, you will be able to identify:

- Critical markets
- Important markets

- Useful markets

- Markets to ignore

Segment	Market Potential		Competitive Advantage	
	Low	High	Low	High
Public Safety	1 2 3 4 5		1 2 3 4 5	
Defense	1 2 3 4 5		1 2 3 4 5	
Utilities	1 2 3 4 5		1 2 3 4 5	
Energy	1 2 3 4 5		1 2 3 4 5	
Construction	1 2 3 4 5		1 2 3 4 5	
Processing Industry	1 2 3 4 5		1 2 3 4 5	
Telecommunications	1 2 3 4 5		1 2 3 4 5	
Multimedia	1 2 3 4 5		1 2 3 4 5	
Components	1 2 3 4 5		1 2 3 4 5	
Private Consumers	1 2 3 4 5		1 2 3 4 5	
Market Channels	Low	High	Low	High
Government	1 2 3 4 5		1 2 3 4 5	
Industrial	1 2 3 4 5		1 2 3 4 5	
Retail/Wholesale	1 2 3 4 5		1 2 3 4 5	
Indirect Distribution	1 2 3 4 5		1 2 3 4 5	
Network Operators	1 2 3 4 5		1 2 3 4 5	
Service Providers	1 2 3 4 5		1 2 3 4 5	
Joint Ventures	1 2 3 4 5		1 2 3 4 5	
Commercial	1 2 3 4 5		1 2 3 4 5	

(These selection criteria are particular to Motorola. Each corporation must incorporate its own portfolio specifics.)

Core Competencies. This part of the analysis defines which core competencies are critical to the country and markets and the degree of their availability. The rating is based on the following parameters:

1 = No competency

2 = Competency anticipated

3 = Competency being developed

4 = Competency available for business segment

5 = Competency in place for entire organization

Competency	Low High
Corporate Culture	1 2 3 4 5
Technology	1 2 3 4 5
Product Portfolio	1 2 3 4 5
Quality	1 2 3 4 5
Cycle Time	1 2 3 4 5
Customer Approach	1 2 3 4 5
Research and Development	1 2 3 4 5
Design/Engineering	1 2 3 4 5
Manufacturing	1 2 3 4 5
Brand Management	1 2 3 4 5
Distribution	1 2 3 4 5
After Sales Support	1 2 3 4 5
Integrated Solutions	1 2 3 4 5
Software Applications	1 2 3 4 5
Program/Project Management	1 2 3 4 5
Network Services	1 2 3 4 5
Frequency Management	1 2 3 4 5
Calibration Procedures	1 2 3 4 5
Financial Management	1 2 3 4 5
Human Resources Management	1 2 3 4 5
Training and Education	1 2 3 4 5
Communications /PR	1 2 3 4 5
Legal/Intellectual Property	1 2 3 4 5

To achieve maximum added value, it is essential to review how the company's core competencies could help overcome the country's deficits and, vice versa, how the countries credentials may be of benefit.

Core competencies do not only apply to strategies, products and services. Customers in emerging markets are often emotional buyers. They prefer what we have to offer because they appreciate the combination of superior product, professional advice and personal relations. The following table highlights some of the essential capabilities of a successful emerging market manager.

Competency	Performance	Potential
Sensitivity to Cultural Diversity	1 2 3 4 5	1 2 3 4 5
Mediator Between Cultures	1 2 3 4 5	1 2 3 4 5
Country Advocate	1 2 3 4 5	1 2 3 4 5
Company Ambassador	1 2 3 4 5	1 2 3 4 5
Custodian of our Key Beliefs	1 2 3 4 5	1 2 3 4 5
Entrepreneur	1 2 3 4 5	1 2 3 4 5
Politically Adept	1 2 3 4 5	1 2 3 4 5
Build Relations	1 2 3 4 5	1 2 3 4 5
Link Opportunities with Capabilities	1 2 3 4 5	1 2 3 4 5
Navigate through Unknown	1 2 3 4 5	1 2 3 4 5
Manage Hardship and Crisis	1 2 3 4 5	1 2 3 4 5
Master Stand-Alone Situations	1 2 3 4 5	1 2 3 4 5
Create Added Value	1 2 3 4 5	1 2 3 4 5
Perseverance and Patience	1 2 3 4 5	1 2 3 4 5

(Using the questionnaire in the Appendix is suggested for collecting the core data indispensable for a market entry decision).

Especially among the first generation of emerging market executives and managers we found many that by far exceeded the above criteria. Here were people, who accepted a difficult task late in their lives. They successfully mastered transition, hardship and crisis. With their enthusiasm they motivated teams and organizations. They turned barriers into opportunities. By doing so, they became role models for future managerial generations.

Strategic Planning Recommendation. Once you have gathered and thoroughly analyzed information from the country exploration, it is time to formulate a strategic planning recommendation. This involves the following steps:

- Developing a vision for the region or country

- Designing a mission for the region or country

- Writing pivotal strategy statements of actions needed to be successful in the region or country

- Developing a set of objectives

- Identifying resources needed to achieve mission, strategies and objectives

- Setting timelines to ensure market exceleration

One of the strategic planning results for Russia was a white paper prepared for the Russian Ministry of Communications. The purpose of this paper was to present a vision of wireless communications in the 21st century, our current spectrum of activities, the possibilities for Russia and a development plan proposal. This plan was composed of the following elements:

1. Consultative services in licensing, type approval, spectrum, standards and telecommunications law

2. Supplier and Driver of leading analog and digital technologies

3. Equipment Manufacturer in an environment of manufacturing excellence

4. Integration of region- and country wide telecommunication systems

5. Operator of wireless services

6. Provider of value-added services such as training and education

Each statement was backed up by roadmaps describing implementation. This 'total systems approach' allowed a structured market entry rather than proceeding in bits and pieces. The Russian partners could work from a concept providing the full range of products, systems and services for upgrading their country. This considerably strengthened our market position.

The Beachhead Concept. Emerging markets are often spread over large territories and physical presence becomes a critical factor. No corporation can afford to establish operations in each emerging market at the same time.

Taking this into account, Motorola applies the beachhead concept. In a given region, a country, which meets most of the criteria for larger territorial coverage, is selected as a beachhead from which the region can best be developed.

This concept may be applied at the beginning of market entry to economize investment and minimize risks. Vice versa, as markets grow and opportunities increase, it may make sense to bundle large regions under one headquarters.

"In the process of regionalization it is important to select the correct locations" comments Eike Bär (General Manager EMEA of a large business unit). "Dubai is a perfect choice as regional hub for the Middle East. By selecting a country, however, which is not on good footing with the target region we may convey a wrong message and jeopardize our own intentions. Such bias may reach far back into history. For some of our activities, we had opened a small headquarters in Russia for the neighbor countries. It created resistance rather than support, because it reactivated old political resentments. The same applies to the selection of the regional manager. A wrong nationality may override all of his or her other credentials." And Eike summarizes, "Regionalization is not only a logistic and infrastructure exercise, but even more so a political process." The following may be of help in determining your location and person:

- Is the location meeting all logistic and infrastructure requirements?

- Is the country in harmony with the countries under the beachhead or regionalization concept or will it evoke resistance?

- If so, is there a balance that still supports our decision or should we better look for another solution?

- Is the considered Regional Manager the right choice in terms of nationality, personality and qualification?

- Do some of his or her credentials outweigh the negative ones (if any) or will it be altogether an unacceptable solution? If so, which alternatives do we have?

A Scenario Planning Case. Nigeria, Ghana, Senegal, Ivory Coast, Chad, Mauritania, Gambia, Liberia and Sierra Leone are countries that could not be more different. Yet, they do have one thing in common: they form the region of West Africa, with 180 million people, which is almost as large as Western Europe. This region, however, is hardly known.

One of our business units wanted to understand the region better in view of already existing but dissipated sales activities and the feeling that there should be more potential. The initiated scenario planning turned out to be most demanding and exerting.

Information gathering was one of the initial hurdles, since readily available data was scarce. This could finally be resolved with the support of key regional experts and international organizations. Another challenge was to convince some of our own staff that this would be a worthwhile exercise in the light of many negative indicators. Once the process started rolling, participants gained an increasing interest, attracted by the high caliber lecturers and the way in which many small puzzle pieces started to form a larger picture.

Here are some of the observations:

- A high political, economic and social diversity

- A wide span between high tier and low tier countries

- Two worlds: the Francophone and the Anglophone countries
- The legacy of colonialism and civil wars (Ivory Coast and others)
- Dominating informal trade (approx. 70%)
- No free movement of labor, capital and goods
- The impact of corruption and bribery
- A shift from old administration to young entrepreneurship
- Plenty of regional development programs
- More opportunities and less risks than expected

As a next step, a regional strategy was developed composed of the following elements:

- Ranking and rating of the countries by their political status

  A: quasi democracies

  B: countries under a dictatorship

  C: those still in a stage of anarchy

- Assessment of the barriers and opportunities
- Design of detailed marketing and sales strategies for the target countries and markets
- Selection of two countries as our beachhead into the region
- Building a relations network taking into account the importance of personal and family ties in Africa

Scenario planning in this and other cases turned out to be an adequate tool for exploring the hidden potential of a region or country which still tends to be overlooked by the world community.

Doing Business in Latin America. Allow us to further elaborate on the scenario planning previously discussed. After having completed such an exercise or other forms of analytical homework formerly unknown territory is converted into a transparent template. This, in turn, will prepare the way to a smooth market entry and unbiased business relations.

Robert Turkovic (Senior Director, Communications and Public Affairs, LAC) describes this mental process on the basis of the Latin American region. He arrives at similar conclusions.

"Latin America is a continent consisting of over 450 million people. The continent itself is several times larger than the United States and Canada put together and is overflowing with multiple cultures, historical backgrounds and peoples. All of this comes together to form the Latin American experience. Originally, indigenous populations inhabited the region, and in the 1500's both Portuguese and Spaniards came to conquer and settle in what they considered as the 'New World'. A unique blend of indigenous, Spanish, Portuguese, African, French, Dutch and Anglo-Saxon cultures came to be rooted in Latin America, where today the predominant languages are Spanish and Portuguese (although Brazilian Portuguese is decidedly different from the Portuguese spoken in Portugal.) The Brazilians do not consider themselves 'Latinos', but for this discussion we will call all nations and their peoples outside of the United States and Canada in the Western hemisphere 'Latin America'.

The traditions of what Anglo-Saxon culture and history has known as the Magna Carta and 'Rights of Man', freedom and equality, came later to Latin America. Indeed, the region was rooted in what may be called 'oaoiquismo' from indigenous times, and later 'caudillisimo' from Spain and Portugal and later transplanted to the Americas in various forms. This concept gave the 'strong armed person' or persons with authority the right to rule a given area. Often these rights were similar to those of a king, who ruled through an army or group of soldiers and/or followers. This was personified by such 'caudillos' coming to power as Ana Maria Lopez de Santa Ana in Mexico, Manuel Rosas in Argentina, and others during the 19th century.

In essence the result of this belief was that trust could only be built upon establishing strong, confident relationships with people. And to this day, this is what rules in Latin America. People in business must get to know one another over an extended period of time, and this may include good and bad times, even in the uncertain economic and political environments in which oftentimes the region is thrust. There has been a rash of military (dictator) regimes during the 20th century amongst them regimes in Cuba, Venezuela and Mexico in the early 20th century, in Argentina, Chile, Haiti and Paraguay and others. Relationship building before entering into a business contract or agreement is what is essential in the region.

Comments have been made on doing business in Latin America during economic, social and political times of uncertainty. I would contend to equate this climate in Latin America as no more unstable, or as unsavory for doing business than some of the following economic, political and social climates that we have found in Europe or Asia, or for that matter in the United States. Witness the communist regimes, and their fall, Bosnia, Serbia and Kosovo, the Asian's economic crisis in the mid 1990's, turmoil in

Northern Ireland, or in the Middle East which continues today, Iraq, Iran, Syria etc. Even September 11th 2001 and the slow economic environment in which we live today in the United States are to be seen in this context.

Why would the region of Latin America be singled out more than any other given the examples above? I tend to think that it is because many of us are unaware of the many positive attributes of this continent."

Country Awareness Programs. The road show proved to be a powerful program for creating instant awareness. Once you have completed the research, it is important to build awareness of your company in the new market. Motorola's key awareness program during market entry is a road show, a two-day event held in major cities of a region to introduce the company to the local key publics and potential customers. For efficiency, we try to capture as many locations within one tour as possible. This requires thorough planning and coordination to move considerable equipment from one place to another within a couple of days and through various borders and customs.

To accommodate audiences of several hundred people, we select large hotels as the venues. The first day includes presentations on the company's organization, culture, products, systems and services. On the second day, participants visit an exhibition where each business has its own booth, and the visitors meet our technical and sales experts. In anticipation of interest in training and development, our programs are displayed in an own booth, which is often overrun by hundreds of students in each city. At the end of each road show, we distribute information in the local language.

The road shows are not only highly effective and successful awareness programs, but they are also unique team-building experiences. A road show team is usually composed of 30 to 50 people, including the Regional Director, business and corporate representatives, secretaries, translators and booth staff. Responsibilities are fluid, and everybody helps where there is a need.

"During the road shows, it was not uncommon for a Motorola colleague to step up to staff an empty booth to answer a visitor's questions," says Shelagh Lester-Smith (Vice President Corporate Communications and Public Affairs). "The response of the visitors and the caliber of the audiences we drew at our events was impressive," Shelagh says. "It was quite common for people to tell us we were the only company that had ever considered putting on a dedicated show in their place. We always got great TV coverage and other good press, and it was not untypical for a minister or mayor to come and see what we were doing."

I can affirm this through one of own experiences. In Moscow, I met a young professor from the Novosibirsk University. He had spent two days and night in the train just to talk to a western company.

Company Week or Day, another country awareness program, is a local event designed for specific target groups. The audience ranges from a group of high-level government officials to a delegation of students from local colleges and universities. The topics are equally diverse and may cover the economic benefits of wireless technology or career perspectives in the telecommunications world of tomorrow. The program is usually coupled with an exhibition of our products and a social event. While the road shows are designed to create initial awareness for large visitor groups, Motorola Week or Day is designed to meet specific expectations and requirements. It also may substitute for a road show, which requires a greater organizational and logistical effort.

The road shows and company days or weeks only make sense in a market exploration phase when a company needs to create initial awareness in an entire region or big country. Participation in fairs and exhibitions might be more economical, although they do not offer the same focus.

As you can see, there are numerous steps involved in the first phase of entering an emerging market. This exploration and pre-startup phase needs comprehensive research and thoughtful, strategic planning. The process also requires defining how the company should present itself in the new marketplace. An equally important step is introducing the company to the new market by building awareness among key customer groups. By doing so, you can prove that are you serious about your mission in the emerging markets.

Chapter 5 - The Startup Phase

Building Local Presence

Once a company has conducted about a year's worth of research and planning, it is ready to enter phase two of the market entry process. During this crucial, one to two-year phase, a company is charged with building the foundation for its success. This means finding the right people and applying the appropriate processes to support its activities in the new market.

During the startup phase, a company should follow these steps:

- Select a legal structure

- Determine the leadership level

- Design an organizational structure

- Register the company

- Lease and facilitate the office establishment

- Hire initial staff

- Establish support functions

- Conduct orientation training

- Set up policies and procedures

- Organize the office opening

- Build a country relations network

Selecting a Legal Structure. In most emerging market countries, there are generally three levels of local presence: the representative or information office, the branch office and the subsidiary. When establishing operations, executives must evaluate these three legal structures to determine which best meets the company's goals in the country. Under some conditions, a corporation may also consider a joint venture with another company. (Of course, there are other legal entities that differ from country to country, but they are too specific for the purposes of this book.)

An overview of the different phases of business establishment is presented in Figure 9.

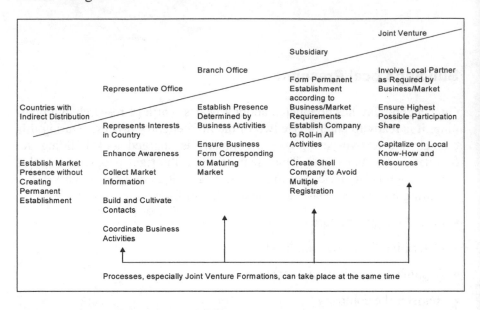

Figure 9: Phases of Business Establishment

The Representative Office is a non-residential and dependent operation hooked up to a legal entity outside the country. The legal impositions in the areas of tax, currency and labor vary greatly. A representative office needs to be registered locally and a legal representation must be appointed. Many corporations select this legal form as a starting platform. An increasing number of countries discourage or even prohibit such offices because they are viewed as a tax shelter. A representative office is usually permitted to perform the following activities:

- Represent its interest in the country

- Enhance awareness and build corporate identity

- Perform market research

- Introduce and promote goods produced by the foreign head office

- Train distributors

- Establish and cultivate contacts to key publics and institutions

- Develop advertising campaigns through local agencies

- Obtain type approvals and influence spectrum allocation

It does not allow the company to:

- Sign sales and purchase contracts with local parties

- Issue billings and invoices to customers

- Hold and handle product inventory

- Partake in the sales of spare parts

- Perform repair and customer services

- Directly hire local personnel

The Branch Office allows a wider range of commercial and technical activities but requires a commercial registration or license and is generally fully taxable. This structure still represents a non-residential and dependent operation and is legally linked to a foreign legal entity. Consequently, the Branch Office does not offer the visibility and leverage of a subsidiary, although it is almost treated as such. Branch Offices are often used as an interim legal structure between a developing and maturing market and are usually replaced by a subsidiary over time.

Of course, the legal status and treatment of Branch Offices may vary considerably by country and cannot be generalized. Countries may have their own special regulations such as in Egypt, where 10 percent of net profits must go toward an employee profit-sharing program.

A subsidiary is a residential independent legal entity in compliance with local company law. This structure may encompass all corporate activities, including capitalization and investments. A subsidiary is frequently used as a shell company to avoid multi-company registration and to accommodate other local operations. As part of its local registration and the appointment of the legal representative-mostly in the function of a general manager-the subsidiary requires the formulation of Articles of Association.

The formation of a joint venture as a commercial activity is possible at any time and independent of other local presence. A joint venture is generally perceived as an agreement between two companies to join forces for a common business purpose with a mutual benefit. For example, a company may capitalize on the local know-how and resources or gain access to a new market segment, while its partner will draw from its expertise and receive financial, logistical and educational support. As a business principle, majority participation above 50 percent should be ensured but some of the emerging market countries only allow minority participation up to 49 percent. Be sure to secure the right to appoint the general manager, the human resources manager and the finance manager in order to maintain business control.

Having been requested to audit one of our joint ventures, I found a basket full of unpleasant surprises. This joint venture did not survive but the mistake had been made up front when we let local management control without supervision.

Under the legal umbrella of Foreign Investment Enterprises, joint ventures in the form of so-called contractual or equity joint ventures are most common in China.

The strategic intent of the corporation will determine which legal structure is most appropriate. A natural approach is to upgrade the organization during the consolidation and expansion phases alongside the market's own maturation. However, business structure and activities may dictate a stronger local presence from the beginning.

In any case it is mandatory to consult the Law Department prior to making a decision. This book can only provide some general guidelines.

Which Leadership Level Is Appropriate? As mentioned in the previous chapter, a company has several leadership options: country manager, business development manager, and branch manager, office manager or similar functions under a different heading. The choice for leadership should reflect the company's strategic intent, as well as the country's structure and potential. Whichever option you choose, it is prudent to hire a candidate with the potential to grow to the next level.

Here are some questions to consider during the leadership selection process:

- Is this a small, middle or large country?

- Is it a low, medium or high opportunity country?

- What level of local presence is projected? How many sectors, groups and divisions?

- What are the forecast sales and headcount numbers?

- Are there any other activities planned besides distribution, such as R&D, manufacturing?

- Is it a virgin market? Or is there already some indirect or direct company presence?

- Does the country already possess a telecommunications infrastructure?

- Does local legislation restrict or favor certain leadership models?

- Is the country expected to become a regional hub later?

Designing the Organizational Structure. Emerging market functions and positions are not stand-alone activities-they are an integrated part of the business and corporate organizations. Nevertheless, it makes sense to present them in a separate organizational scheme for a strong market focus and as a clear reference for outsiders. While each company needs to design a structure that fits its organizational need, Motorola came up with the following five-layer scheme:

1. Global Business and Corporate Level. This first layer comprises the individual business and corporate functions outside the country

2. Regional Management Level. This second layer is composed of the Regional Directors

3. Regional Corporate Support Level. The third layer consists of the support functions outside the country

4. Country Management Level. The fourth layer embraces the Country Manager, Business Development Manager and Branch Manager

5. Country Business and Corporate Level. The fifth level includes all local functions of the sectors, groups, divisions and corporate office that are present in the country

In compliance with Motorola's overriding structure, all functions and positions at each layer report directly to their higher-level counterpart and only indirectly to the Country Management and Regional Director. The only exception is Country Management, which reports directly to the Regional Director. Figure 10 portrays these levels in a comprehensive form.)

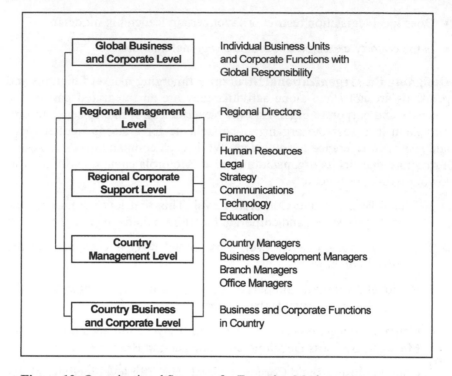

Global Business and Corporate Level	Individual Business Units and Corporate Functions with Global Responsibility
Regional Management Level	Regional Directors
Regional Corporate Support Level	Finance Human Resources Legal Strategy Communications Technology Education
Country Management Level	Country Managers Business Development Managers Branch Managers Office Managers
Country Business and Corporate Level	Business and Corporate Functions in Country

Figure 10: Organizational Structure for Emerging Markets

Company Registration. Registering of an office or subsidiary varies considerably from country to country. Generally, the process takes between three and six months, but occasionally it may be more extended and complicated.

All registration documents need to be translated, notarized and supernotarized. It is crucial to use the services and know-how of a local law firm or the affiliate of a Western legal office. Since the cycle time at consulates, embassies and other authorities can be lengthy, it is prudent to start the registration process at the very beginning. For this reason, it has become common practice to collect all relevant documents during the first explorative field trip and complete them gradually, as plans become more solid. Typical delays involve questions about the office or subsidiary name, last minute changes of the office structure, document renewal requirements and simple logistics, such as slow mail.

Over time, our legal departments developed considerable expertise in handling registrations. Here are some of the major steps within the process:

- Obtain registration documents from a local or Western source (law firm, public accountants, embassy)

- Determine appropriate legal structure based on business intent (representative or branch office, or subsidiary)

- Propose and appoint a legal representative (country or business development manager)

- Select carrier for registration (local law firm, affiliate of foreign legal office)

- Identify company name and verify its appropriateness with local experts

- Locate approving authorities (usually Ministry of Commerce)

- Prepare documents (translation, notarization, super-notarization) and submit them to authorities

- Establish company by-laws

- Open local bank account and obtain bank guarantee if needed

- Pay registration fees and inform management and businesses upon completion

- Provide proper legal content and layout for stationery and business cards

Many corporations report that legislation proves to be particularly complex in China. It usually involves the following steps:

- Preparing a feasibility study

- Obtaining project approval

- Defining a joint venture agreement

- Issuing a business license

Certain countries in Latin America promote the easy formulation of short-term companies, which cease to exist when a defined project has been concluded.

The Selection and Facilitation of Offices. It was late night in Prague. I was sitting awake in my hotel room and was in big trouble. We had lost our office on short notice. The office grand opening was only four weeks away, and more than 500 invitations had already been sent. How did this happen?

In Prague, there was no adequate office space available in the early '90s because property rights were vague and there was no new construction. I had looked at about 30 places from overpriced villas to dull apartments. Finally, I found out that the city administration had plans to sublease parts of its office building adjacent to the downtown theater. We filed a letter of intent, but from there on we did not hear anything despite several follow-up calls. Finally, I received a warning from another potential tenant that the building had been withdrawn from the market. Then the truth came to light: The ground on which the theater was built belonged to the church and was confiscated by the communists. The church had taken the case to court and it was not yet resolved. Fortunately, we found another building a few days later, and we celebrated the office opening even though it was not ready.

This story illustrates the office situation in the early years. New constructions were rare, and renovated older buildings were very expensive. We quickly found out that we were safe when dealing with landlords of big multinational companies or with local governments. By contrast, some entrepreneurs considered this market a source for making quick money. For instance, a landlord asked us to put a million-dollar deposit in a bank account in the Bahamas. Usually, however, we were successful in identifying and leasing quality offices offering functionality, flexibility and adequate space at a fair price in a good environment. This was even less complicated in Latin America, the Asia region and in the Middle East because there were plenty of excellent buildings and a well-developed infrastructure.

The project of establishing a new office is in the hands of a small team of experts from human resources and facility management, legal, finance, security and electronic data processing (EDP) system support, according to Margret Klemann (Manager Employee Relations and Facilities). Facility management and HR staff were usually the point people in a new country. "It took up to three visits before we had pulled the various pieces together and a final concept was ready," Margret says.

In the due diligence tests preceding each lease, we rated a number of factors (see following chart). These criteria only apply to sales-oriented offices and subsidiaries. More complex and stringent criteria need to be developed from case to case for R&D, manufacturing, service and other operational facilities.

Facilities Rating Tool

Building/Office	Rating Inadequate Adequate
Is the building old, renovated or new?	1 2 3 4 5
How is the building quality and maintenance?	1 2 3 4 5
Which environment is the building located in: industrial, housing, city, suburb?	1 2 3 4 5
Who is the landlord: private, public, other company?	1 2 3 4 5
Is the landlord open or reserved to our specific requirements?	1 2 3 4 5
Are the lease terms and conditions in line with the market practice?	1 2 3 4 5
Does the building structure and layout meet our needs?	1 2 3 4 5
Is the office space functional and flexible for growth and modification?	1 2 3 4 5
Is the safety and security standard commensurate to our policies and local needs?	1 2 3 4 5
What are the other tenants: local, multinational, competition?	1 2 3 4 5
When will the office be available and how much facilitation is needed up front?	1 2 3 4 5
Can we put a corporate sign on the roof and a logo on the entrance?	1 2 3 4 5
What is the public image of the building and the landlord?	1 2 3 4 5
Are our top management and businesses in agreement with the office?	1 2 3 4 5

Concurrent with the office search, facility management starts the process of locating adequate suppliers and craftsmen, checking their qualifications and obtaining quotes. This pertains to:

- Office furniture
- Office machinery and equipment
- Conference room furniture and equipment
- Kitchen appliances
- Telecommunications
- Local area network (LAN)

- Computerization

- Construction upgrading

- Carpeting, wallpaper, curtains

- Security installations, etc.

"In the early years there was a critical shortage of local suppliers," Margret says. "We had to import most furniture and equipment from adjacent countries. Delivery and cycle times, customs procedures and transportation required patience, improvisation and perseverance. To become operational, we carried loads of office stationary in our own suitcases." In one case, Margret had to spend two days at the German-Polish border to ensure that our truckload of office furniture was processed through customs and not stolen. The more local suppliers became available, the more we switched to a 'buy local' policy to demonstrate our local commitment and benefit from local service and warranties.

The availability of local area networks (LAN) is one of the most essential elements for any new office. Sometimes, in the initial years, an office startup plan was not synchronized with the telecommunications organization, and the facility could not communicate with the counterparts outside the country.

"Some countries were a difficult territory for us because of the lack of infrastructure, suppliers, equipment and customer orientation," says K.Y. Chiu (Director Emerging Markets Systems Support). He identifies a number of opportunities and barriers:

- Internal information sharing

- Infrastructure readiness in the country

- Relationship with telecommunications authorities

- Import and export process

- Sourcing and pricing of computer hardware and software

- Local vendor support

- Office system standards

- Standard operating procedures and documentation

- Project management

For many EDP departments this presented a bottleneck in the start-up. It therefore became critical to tag this subject with a red flag in the start-up plan.

Once an office is leased and furniture vendors have been identified, a special appropriation request is prepared. Requiring approval by top management, this request details the occupation plan, financial investment requirements and cost allocation among the businesses. It also forms the basis for a detailed action plan, which is executed under the supervision of facility management.

Figure 11 portrays this detailed action plan.

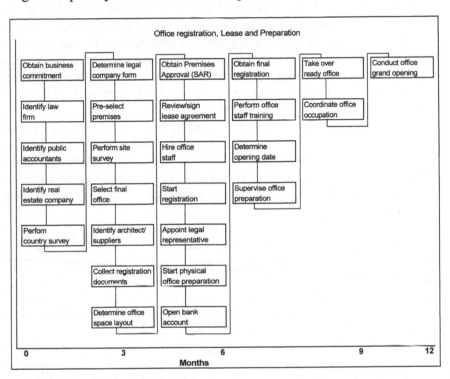

Figure 11: Mapping of Time Frames

Establishing a More Complex Operation. As mentioned before, other criteria apply to establishing a more complex operation. They include R&D, manufacturing, assembly, installation, maintenance, repair, service and other functions.

A planning error that requires management to reverse a decision and relocate or shut-down a major operation will generate a much higher impact on image, timeframe and cost than in the case of a small office. A large-scale exodus from an emerging market may close that door forever. Therefore, establishing a local presence has to be thought of as a long-term commitment to the region.

The Origin of Present Infrastructures. Geographically, the old civilizations congregated around the early trading routes. Like pearls on a necklace they served as bearers of economic development and formed the nucleus of the present infrastructures in many world regions. Merchants, craftsmen, pirates, robbers, smugglers, soldiers and artists also used them for their travel purposes.

Many of the old connections still exist and have developed over time into the current centers of trade. One of the most famous routes was the Silk Route linking China with Europe and transporting the Asian culture and goods into Europe. It is currently experiencing an unexpected renewal since Azerbaijan is building a pipeline alongside the old Route to transport their oil into the West. Another ancient route is the Incense Route starting in Oman and connecting the Orient with the Occident.

These routes were not just simple streets, but were composed of a network of side routes, junctions and assembly points similar to a computer diagram. They also functioned as melting pots for civilizations. If you compare your business location in one of the world trade centers with the old maps, you may find yourself in the middle of an ancient network, what an exciting thought.

Staff Recruitment. The initial office staff typically consists of the office head - the country-, business development- or branch manager -, a secretary, a driver and some business representatives. The driver takes care of many outside activities such as mail, messenger services, driving the staff, maintaining the company cars and more. In the United Arab Emirates, this is a legally prescribed function called "Mr. Fix-it."

For the efficiency of any start up organization, we were well advised in recruiting candidates with the potential for higher level tasks. A secretary with office management skills and a driver with logistical capabilities are most helpful when keeping to a budget and covering a large spectrum of typical start up activities. Companies that thought they could do away with "Mr. Fix-it" tended to get lost in the jungle of local bureaucracy.

Before initiating any recruitment, it is important to:

- Perform local benchmarking of compensation, benefits and employment terms

- Obtain or prepare job descriptions and job grades in accordance with the relevant corporate structure

- Design standard hiring procedures and contracts based on both external and internal inputs

- Determine recruitment resources (internal job opportunity program, local newspaper advertising, search firms, universities, word of mouth)

- Advertise open positions, organize and conduct interviews, extend employment offers to final candidates and complete employment contracts

- Procure export control clearance for sensitive positions and countries in compliance with US Government and corporate policies

- Integrate new hires into local payroll and office organization

- Organize and conduct orientation training for new employees

This checklist sounds like a job description for recruiters, yet there is more to it. Local hiring practices may differ greatly from our standards and need to be adjusted very specifically. For managerial and professional jobs, we have been successful in generating internal candidates, ideally people who work in the Western world but have local roots. A few times, we found some employees were not well accepted in their home countries-those who had endured the pain did not always welcome those who returned only after the worst was over.

In the recruitment process, we were frequently faced with our expectations that were higher than the qualifications provided. This could be partially compensated by the overwhelming motivation of staff to do a good job. The more Western corporations flooded into the markets, the lower the number of qualified candidates for positions became. Oversaturated labor markets such as in Singapore found innovative solutions e.g. outsourcing work to adjacent low cost countries. Bureaucratic hurdles also occasionally aggravated recruitment. Hiring personnel for a representative office in China, for instance, necessitated a working plan to be submitted to a Foreign Service Company, which acted as a recruitment agency charging high fees.

The Corporate Support Functions. The following corporate support functions serve the emerging markets:

- Finance

- Human Resources

- Legal

- Security

- Facilities

- Strategy

- Communications

- Information Technology

Support may be rendered from outside the country or locally. The statutory requirements of a subsidiary may call for local support upon its foundation. Finance and Human Resources are usually the first functions established locally, though a burning governmental issue may dictate the need for local government relations at an early stage.

A key factor is the critical mass of the office. This may be defined by sales volume, headcount, complexity of the environment, country legislation and other factors. While our first approach was to hold back on local support until such a critical mass was reached, we now offer local support much earlier in the process. Experience has taught us that once you miss an opportunity, you are always in a reactive instead of proactive mode. This can be detrimental to organizational efficiency and local compliance.

Orientation Training. Familiarizing our newly hired managers and employees with a company's history, culture, portfolios, organization and activities is an important part of the startup phase. How can we expect new hires to inherit our values if they are not properly trained?

We put a high priority on a thorough training process delivered in a specific sequence. One of the key elements is the introductory training that occurs within the first three months of employment.

Mirka Wojnar reports that the interest level of new employees was so high that she was almost unable to handle all their questions. And frequently, employees who have been on board for some time register for the program as well. Whenever training is offered in some of our Western organizations, often only 70 of 80 registered participants make it. By contrast, whenever training is offered in Asia classes are frequently overbooked, and people even attend spontaneously without prior registration because they want to learn.

Setting Up the Policies and Procedures. In emerging markets, the availability of a complete set of policies and procedures is even more vital than in mature countries for three reasons. First, we hire large numbers of locals who have never faced such a complexity of rules and regulations in a foreign business culture. Second, many of our original policies and procedures cannot be used since they do not match the local culture, processes and language. A third element is time. At the beginning, we made the error of thinking that this task was not urgent since there were only a few employees. Soon, we were overtaken by the speed of the established local presence. We fell behind at a moment that was critical for new employees, who needed guidance but were often left alone. Therefore, the following rules should become elementary policy in each organization and corporation entering an emerging market country:

- Have your policies and procedures in place and your "human resources act" together before hiring employees

- Adjust your rules and regulations to the local environment but without giving up your principles

- Have your material translated into the local language by a local translator in close cooperation with a corporate policy and procedures expert

- Train your local employees

- Don't overdo the training-a few pages with the most important key issues are much more efficient than loads of detailed publications

- Create a system to adjust policies and procedures to fast-changing legislation

- Ensure full compliance with local legislation, and don't leave it up to your people to decide which position to take

The Office Grand Opening. Grand openings for new offices are an outstanding way to build awareness. They are viewed as a unique opportunity to present the company and its local investment to a large audience of VIPs from government, industry, commerce, education, media, and Western companies and institutions.

The keynote speakers are typically CEOs, local ministers and US ambassadors. Accommodating up to several hundred guests, the event is usually held in a historical or cultural venue, coupled with entertainment, and wining and dining. In the local media, the opening ceremonies are covered as a high-class event.

A grand opening requires as much as six months of thorough planning and preparation. The most important step is to identify the key players, get their titles and names right and invite them with ample lead-time.

Building a Country Relations Network. Network building is the corner-stone of market exceleration. Some of the best resources are the contacts gained in the exploration phase and during the office grand opening. Another efficient, though seldom used, leverage is the network of major export countries, for example, Great Britain in the former Commonwealth, France in North and West Africa, and Germany in Central and Eastern Europe. Also, memberships in associations are inexpensive and highly effective. A dinner with a fellow member may open the door to new opportunities.

The following is a short list of primary contacts in emerging market countries:

- Ministry of Commerce

- Ministry of Interior

- Technical Ministries

- Chamber of Commerce

- Business associations

- Western embassies

- Western consulates

- Trade associations

- Employers' associations

- Universities, dean's offices and relevant faculties

- Local colleges

- American universities

- Local and Western law firms

- Public accountants

- Company distributors

- Multinational companies

- Employees already in the country

Sometimes, even some of the former or existing networks may be helpful. Here are two examples:

The Asian Diasporas. The South Asian and Chinese Diasporas are powerful organizations accounting for over 50 million members. They operate perfectly organized global networks and are hubs of political, social and business links up to the highest levels throughout the world. Not only do they manufacture and distribute goods; they also hold a tremendous asset portfolio of foreign property, investments and citizenship rights.

The Hapsburg Dynasty. The former Hapsburg dynasty is another of the permanent old connections. In the Middle Ages it became the greatest political power in Europe, consisting of 30 million people of German, Czech, Slovakian, Polish, Croatian, Slovenian, Italian, Hungarian and Austrian origin (amongst other minorities.) Although dissolved after World War I, the old connections proved to be particularly helpful in the Cold War for mastering the common fate and constructing a mental barrier against communism. With regards to contemporary business, the former networks were of value to Western business people when entering these markets after 1990.

Another source of information is those institutions and organizations, which were formed to promote regional development. (See Appendix "Regional Organizations and Institutions").

Involve Your Distributor. It is also prudent to involve the company's agents and distributors as early as possible in the process to inform them of your plans and make it clear that you do not intend to build a competitive situation, but rather a complementary strategy. By doing so, you gain friends who help you open doors. Otherwise, you risk making enemies who can put a lot of roadblocks in your way.

The steps you take in the startup phase strengthen the framework of your new business. The process involves cultivating the best partners, employees and resources to follow up your entry in to the new market. It also takes thoughtful planning to set up the proper training functions and corporate policies that support your mission in the market. Completing this process requires balancing your resources back home with building up your critical mass at the local level. Once you have completed this process, you are ready to move on to the next phase of the process, consolidation.

Chapter 6 - The Consolidation Phase

After a company has built a local presence and made a name for itself in an emerging market, it is ready to tackle the consolidation phase, which may take up to two years. In the consolidation phase, a company has good experiences with the following programs:

- Upgrade the local presence

- Establish the country council

- Prepare the Memorandum of Understanding (MOU)

- Human resource development

- Organizational integration

Upgrading the Local Presence

Upgrading the local presence takes place horizontally and vertically through an organization. Across the horizontal structure of a company, the process embraces activities beyond sales and marketing: R&D, manufacturing, service and support centers, etc. Up and down the vertical structure of a company, the process means shifting to a higher level legal structure: from a representative to a branch office, or from a branch office to a subsidiary. During the consolidation phase, most corporate support functions will already be in place locally, as discussed in the previous chapter.

The Country Council. This originates from the major Western European countries, Germany, France and Great Britain, where it became necessary to supplement the business structure with another level representing the country. The purpose of the country council is to promote the company in the country and handle issues that cannot be tackled by the individual businesses or that require a concerted approach.

An exemplary charter of a country council, under the leadership of the country manager and the attendance of the local managers of the businesses and corporate functions, should include the following scope of activities:

- Develop a country plan derived from the individual business plans
- Create a favorable environment for business activities
- Improve political effectiveness and public image
- Coordinate certain key accounts in which more than one business is involved
- Proactively pursue legislative and regulatory issues
- Drive organizational and management programs
- Enhance corporate identity and unity of purpose
- Intensify cohesion and communications among the businesses in the country
- Obtain maximum leverage from the company's overall presence

The charter may differ from country to country depending on the specific environment and on the maturity of the local team. It has proven to be particularly useful in large territories with remote locations, where the country council is the only platform for regular joint meetings of the widely dispersed organizations. The council usually meets three or four times per year.

The Memorandum of Understanding. A powerful tool for the local team is the Memorandum of Understanding (MOU) usually a document of a few pages describing the country vision and mission, key strategic areas and action plans for the next 12 months. This binding document is developed, agreed upon, signed and implemented by the local country team. Here is a sample of the MOU process in Poland:

Vision:

Earn recognition of customers, employees, suppliers, shareholders and the Polish community as a premier company in the country:

- With local roots, presence, impact, respect, innovation and leadership
- Contributing to the growth and development of Poland
- Committed to the future of Poland

Mission:

- Be an engine of growth for the company's sales and profits
- Balance strong business imperatives with country imperatives to maximize and enhance business success
- Create strong awareness and value for the corporate brand
- Create presence and value that enhances the effectiveness of Poland's national development and the company's worldwide performance

Key Strategic Areas:

- Understand the Polish government's development strategy and coordinate a response to influence it (e.g., in wireless communications)
- Develop and implement plans for new investment in software development, component manufacture, R&D, education and other manifestations of the company's long-term commitment to Poland, and market these investments with Polish constituencies
- Discover and match the company's specific needs, business by business, to talents that are uniquely available in the Polish labor market and continue/initiate recruitment activities for the best students in Polish universities
- Commit to work together as a team in pursuing the vision of the company in Poland

Author's note: Many action items were identified, formulated and agreed upon but are not listed here because they are too specific for the purpose of this book.

The response to the MOU was very different in South Africa. I remember facilitating the local team there while it was identifying which key issues would become part of their MOU. At the beginning of the brainstorming session, participants were rather skeptical and reserved. Then the atmosphere slowly warmed up, and at the end, everyone felt satisfied that they had worked together on a job well done. These are the key country issues they identified, and these were subsequently shaped into an MOU format:

- Brand awareness   Shared resources
- Promotion of education   Manufacturing
- Quality initiatives   Positioning as local supplier

- Image
- Rural development
- Import duties
- Southern Africa strategy
- Local partnering
- Product awareness
- Affirmative action
- Consolidated distribution
- High-level government relations
- University/ college relations
- Community relations

Regionalization

Security

Other company local presence

Communications (people and systems)

Efficient office operations

Cross-border interface

Targeting new markets/opportunities

Risk assessment/crisis management

Awareness/upwards communications

Sharing experiences/learning

Country council

A program called "Score Card" recently amended the Memorandum of Understanding.

Human Resources Development. Once a local organization and its staff have reached a certain maturity, it is appropriate to integrate them into the corporation's human resources development schemes. This will be of mutual benefit. For the employees, it opens the door to a structured development of their potential, while the company gains access to untapped human resources.

A career path under communism was dictated by the Party interests and the person's willingness to comply with the system. Many employees in the public sector climbed up the political ladder and ended up at their highest level of inefficiency. Only those with outstanding intellectual capabilities and achievements were granted a small sense of freedom, as in the case of famous artists and scientists with a high reputation in the West.

For many of our local managers and employees exposure to a performance management system was like a rebirth. They had never experienced goal setting, performance measurement, pay for performance and a structured career scheme. One night, I received a phone call at home from one of our Russian employees. Very excited, he apologized for disturbing me about a very pressing matter. His supervisor had asked him to collect his input for an upcoming performance review. He asked me if he was being fired for doing something wrong. I calmed him down and explained the misunderstanding as well as I could. Apparently, the invitation to a one-on-one meeting in the communist world spelled bad news.

Similarly, East Germans who started working in our factories after the fall of communism reported high stress. They were not used to working eight hours consecutively without major interruptions. In their former manufacturing plants, inventory shortages caused frequent work stoppages.

In the Middle East, we encountered a different kind of cultural diversity. Many questions common in Western performance reviews are taboo because a local citizen is uncomfortable disclosing such details to a foreigner.

In Asia traditional personal relationships had brought about a management style built on a hierarchical structure, collective decision making and the striving for compromises and harmony.

In the light of these diversities, the adjustment of human resources development schemes became a rather sensitive task.

Organizational Integration. In countries or regions with several company locations, organizations drift apart easily and rapidly. We see this in some advanced countries that have so many diversified business locations and activities that they don't even know each other. While this may be tolerable in a market where the company is well known, it is a weakness in emerging markets where one-stop shopping is critical to an efficient startup.

This is particularly true in a large territory. There, the widely dispersed organizations must communicate and meet with each other to exchange their good and bad experiences, and the country council helps hold the strings together.

> *During the consolidation phase, a company will refine its operations and upgrade its presence. It can also take important steps to integrate some of its operations, thus building a more unified front. These steps are critical for a company to undertake before it moves on to the fourth phase of entering an emerging market, maintenance and expansion. In the next chapter, we'll learn more about what it takes to bring a company to this final stage of market entry.*

Chapter 7 - The Maintenance and Expansion Phase

Enlarging the Local Platform

Once a company has consolidated its operations in an emerging market, it enters the final phase of market penetration, the maintenance and expansion phase. In this phase, which usually begins after five years in the country, the company follows these process steps:

- Expand the organization
- Upgrade support infrastructure
- Adjust policies and procedures
- Regionalize
- Provide job enrichment
- Reintegrate

Expanding the Organization. In the early years, the interest level for entering an emerging market was rather low. We had to work hard to get buy-in from our businesses. Once we overcame the initial hurdles, the local organizations were able to master the preliminary exploration and startup phases. Then the potential of these countries surfaced, businesses developed, and they were pressed to provide the infrastructure for their local presence. This quantitative influx was accompanied by a qualitative increase of local functions such as R&D, joint ventures, assembly and service and support centers.

These expansive activities required a great amount of discipline at all managerial levels in order to not lose the momentum built up in the initial phase and miss out on the benefits of the channeled and structured start-up activities.

Upgrade Support Infrastructure. This runs alongside the above expansion measures. In some regions, the growth and complexity of the operation may, therefore, warrant localizing some corporate functions to support regional efficiency and autonomy. Of course, it is important not to lose sight of their affordability and economies of scale to avoid becoming bloated, inefficient organizations.

Adjust Policies and Procedures. Even though it is sometimes difficult to change a policy because people have become comfortable with it, we must regularly review our policies and procedures. Now that we are more knowledgeable about a country or region, are the policies and procedures suitable? Are they still meeting the requirements in a fast-changing environment? This, of course, does not include our principal policies, such as the code of conduct and the standards of internal control. Yet there are piles of standard operating procedures (SOPs) that have become obsolete or need to be revised. Some of them are even superfluous, such as an anti-alcohol policy in the Middle East where alcohol is forbidden by religion.

Regionalize. Regionalization is a helpful management tool to deal with large territories and to maximize efforts. This principle has already been discussed under the heading "The Beachhead Concept", see Chapter 4.

Provide Job Enrichment. The more a country develops and the greater the organizational efficiency becomes, the more likely the capabilities of the Country Manager or Business Development Manager will outgrow their initial responsibilities. The next step would then logically be to appoint someone to take over operational responsibility for a major business or key account. This can only be a win-win situation: The business or key account will benefit from the incumbent's in depth knowledge about the country. He or she, in turn, will benefit from the opportunity to climb the career ladder. As a positive side effect continuity of business will also be retained for the country. For this position Motorola created the job title of "Business Leader."

Re-integrate. This is the current strategy applied by Motorola in some countries. Once a corporation is settled in the emerging markets, which have by their own efforts now reached a stable, mature position, its organizational concept should be reviewed. It might be appropriate to dissolve the start-up organization and re-integrate it into the corporations' larger structure. Reasons for such an action may be economies of scale, organizational streamlining, or simply a return to the business day to day routine. It is important in a re-integration process to make sure that individual and collective know-how acquired in the start-up process does not get lost. Properly recording all experiences and results is essential to ensure this. If these invaluable experiences are adequately preserved and documented, they may be quickly re-activated in the case of new emerging market entries.

Figure 12 summarizes the four phases of market entry.

Phase 1:

Exploration and Pre-Startup

Appoint Champion

Determine Positioning Strategy

Obtain Top Management Commitment

Form Exploration Team

Establish Selection Criteria

Prioritize Countries

Develop Strategic Recommendation

Run Country Awareness Programs

Phase 3:

Consolidation

Upgrade Presence

Invest in Local Support

Establish Country Council and MOU

Develop Human Resources

Integrate Operations

Phase 2:

Startup

Select Legal Form

Determine Leadership Level

Design Organization structure

Lease and Facilitate Office

Hire Initial Staff

Set up Policies and Procedures

Establish Support Functions

Organize Office Opening

Build Country Relations Network

Phase 4:

Maintenance/Expansion

Expand Organization

Upgrade Support Infrastructure

Adjust Policies and Procedures

Implement Regionalization

Provide Job Enrichment

Re-integrate

Figure 12: Emerging Market Entry Model

The Effects of Unstable Markets

Regions, countries and markets occasionally tend not to follow the pattern of the business phases described. Macro-economic and political conditions may overrule structural processes and present completely new scenarios as we have seen in the book before. Corporations and business people are faced with the bitter truth that the only constant is change; and they may find themselves thrown back from the end to the beginning of market entry. A prime example is Latin America with its ongoing ups and downs. Carlos Genardini (President, LAC Region) describes the story of telecommunications in the context of an unstable environment and its impact on corporations.

Ups and Downs in Latin America. "The Latin America and Caribbean market has a history of saw tooth economic cycles of fast growth and prosperity followed by high inflation and currency devaluation. In spite of the peaks and valleys the region's economy grows at an annual rate of 3%. The 1990's were representative of fast economic growth and new technology building hopes of revitalizing the region. For the 450 million inhabitants jobs were being created and their pleas for improved telecommunications systems and services were being addressed. They were on the cusp of joining the 20th century technology and service boom. By the end of the decade global companies like Portugal Telecom, Telecom Italia and Telefonica amongst other European companies were heavily investing along with Bell South, Bell Canada and SBC in this region. The Europe 2G and 3G licensing bonanza fueled the minds of regulators with new levels of revenue for Latin American countries.

Motorola invested in a significant manufacturing capability in Brazil and established software centers throughout the region complimenting the sales, marketing and business teams serving the region. We were poised to serve our customers.

By 2002, it was obvious that the economies were over heated, the political scene rapidly changing and the bubble of 3G licenses had burst. The end result was a new cycle of inflation and devaluing currencies. Regardless of how bad business was the number of cellular users continued to increase thanks to prepaid methodologies but lowered the average revenue per user to all time lows.

The region continues to build its telecommunications systems and focus on optimizing what they have. Mergers and acquisitions are in the news with companies like Americas Movil, which have become the major wireless operator by doing so. Motorola, like other organizations, significantly had to downsize its capability, rebuild its presence in the region and reposition itself for the next up cycle."

The Long Walk in China

"The Phoenix is a legendary bird that thrives on brilliance. It is an auspicious creature that symbolizes happiness and prosperity because it only nests in places where the future holds promise. The open door and economic reform policies initiated by the Chinese Government in the late 1970's turned a page in China's history and paved the way for modernization, growth and prosperity. Now, major corporations on the world stage could also avail themselves of unprecedented opportunities afforded by these policies and by the support of the Chinese people who welcomed their arrival. As a phoenix soars towards the sun, Motorola was attracted to China, where tremendous modernization has been leading the country to prosperity and abundance. Encouraged by its will to succeed, rich resources, diligent and hospitable people and booming economy, Motorola chose to make this country a second home."

This strategy statement, written in the symbolic language of the local culture, manifests Motorola's ultimate commitment to China. Its implementation turned out to become a lengthy, complex process with many ups and downs. We have put this business case at the end of this chapter because it confirms many elements of the four phase model. Certainly, this exciting story will sound familiar to many other investors entering China in the early days.

Motorola's activities in China started in the early 1960's. In 1967 the company set up its first manufacturing plant in Hong Kong. This was followed by the installation of 2 way radio systems at various customs authorities in 1981/82. Our first representative office was opened in Beijing in 1987.

A breakthrough was achieved in 1986 when Bob Galvin visited China and the door was opened to mutual partnerships and substantial local investment. In 1992 our first legal entity was founded in Beijing. These are a few of the milestones, which Motorola was proud to celebrate in 1997, its tenth anniversary in China.

Chi Sun Lai, Motorola's first country manager and later on first president in China accepted this assignment in 1988. Having lived in the United States and worked for Motorola, he was aware of the adverse circumstances that were awaiting him. Yet, his desire to help his country and its people and to enable Motorola to establish a local presence waived all his concerns and the hurdles on the way. It was indeed a long walk from the first few tentative steps to the present leading position in the electronics field.

The official contacts started in a climate of mutual caution. Initially, the Chinese government perceived Motorola as just one more of those Western companies, which want to take quick advantage of their potential. Motorola, in turn, viewed China as an unstable political and economic environment with investment at risk. Meanwhile, Motorola launched a multi-million USD investment into local operations, infrastructure and human resources, while in the People's Congress the cooperation of the two partners was officially appreciated as an example of how China can succeed in the global economy.

The decade in between was filled with mutual trust and relations building involving the highest ruling executives and government officials on both sides. The starting point was one of the early senior executive programs (SEP) which had instituted an Asian Pacific Task Force to investigate opportunities in the region. This was supplemented later on by a China Task Force.

Motorola's concern was that it would be forced to form a joint venture where the Chinese partners would have control of the process and we would be limited in implementing all the programs which distinguish us as a leading technologist, premier employer and good citizen. And the Chinese officials feared that the benefits for their country would be rather limited if they let a foreign company control the business.

By tracing back the history of telecommunications, Motorola finally recognized that risks had always been generally much lower and opportunities much higher than expected. The Chinese government anticipated that they would limit themselves in upgrading their country if they did not remove some of the barriers. This change was supported by new provisions for foreign investors passed by the Chinese government in the mid 80's and aiming at considerable alleviation for investment and trade. As a result, and in appreciation of the high investment and path of growth, Motorola was the only global corporation at that time which was allowed to be set-up as a wholly owned subsidiary.

The student riots in Beijing exposed mutual relations to a hardship test. Shi Sun Lai and his team managed to keep up the mutual dialogue. It was mainly his merit that Motorola did not pull out like it had been forced to do in South Africa whilst major competitors left China.

After these events, things turned for the better, which even allowed Motorola to take a firm position on human rights. In the meantime both parties have created a close and intense relationship, which feels like a second home.

The strategy endorsed for the new century predestines China as a global base for many of Motorola's future activities.

Once a business has investigated ways to expand, upgrade and regionalize, it is well positioned to maintain and grow its presence in an emerging market. With the four phases complete, a company should have a solid, local presence that can adapt to the market's needs while staying true to the corporate mission back home.

Chapter 8 - Added Value of Market Entry Strategies

Throughout all phases of market entry, a high benefit was derived designing so-called added value strategies. They fulfill several purposes:

- Create market-entry models that overcome initial barriers and provide a competitive position.

- Enable a two-way transfer of knowledge where the country may capitalize on Motorola's expertise and we may benefit from the country's resources.

- Develop partnerships and alliances to promote opportunities that contribute to mutual success and welfare.

Parviz Mokhtari (Director, CEE / MEA) led the process of designing these strategies. He says the situation in Central and Eastern Europe was so unique that our classical strategy portfolio did not provide all the recipes we needed. "We actually had to reinvent ourselves and conceive a new strategy, taking into account that both the countries and ourselves started from a zero base," Parviz says. "Fortunately enough, our top management left us a lot of freedom, and we did not have to go through many decision levels since everything was new for everybody. So we started with a blank sheet of paper, and we were able to set a direct course for the goal."

The overriding strategy was added value. Parviz's team identified four strategic fields. At the same time, each sector, group and division developed its own strategies focusing on its business plans and market segments. To minimize overlapping and performance gaps, corporate functions and businesses regularly coordinated their strategies.

The Strategic Fields

The four strategic fields the team identified were to:

1. Leverage our strengths

2. Shift resources into the country

3. Enhance its premier employer and good citizen role

4. Promote synergy and corporate identity

These are seen graphically in Figure 13 below.

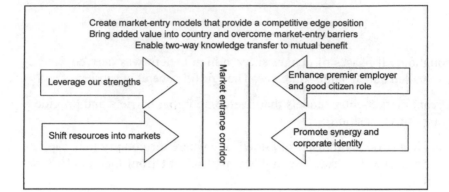

Figure 13: Added Value Strategies

Leverage Our Strengths

- Technology platforms

- Advanced products, systems and services

- Spectrum management expertise

- Quality improvement

- Cycle-time reduction

- Total customer satisfaction

- Training and education

- Market-entry programs

- Supplier and distributor qualification

- Financing solutions for customers

These strategies enable the country to gain access to the technological and management know-how of a market leader, acquire a state-of-the-art product portfolio and receive support in the development of policy and infrastructure. The company, in turn, will deal with a new dimension of partners who will achieve a higher level of sophistication.

Shift Resources into the Country

- Offices and subsidiaries

- Joint ventures

- Alliances and Cooperation

- Centers of excellence (R&D, software)

- Agent and distributor network

- Assembly and manufacturing

- Supplier base

- In-country events

Bringing these resources into a new market will generate investment and employment for the country. The company will be able to achieve a faster, more intense market penetration and build close relationships with key publics.

Enhance Premier Employer and Good Citizen Role

- Employment and career opportunities

- Attractive employment terms and conditions

- Educational partnerships with universities and colleges

- Undergraduate and graduate programs

- Educational support and donations

- Community events and sponsorships

- Compliance with local culture and customs

In view of the cultural diversity in the emerging markets, this will initiate a mutually rewarding cultural exchange. It will allow us to become an accepted member of the local community. The local workforce will be integrated into our global employment and career opportunities while the company will gain access to untapped human resources.

Promote Synergy and Corporate Identity

- Shared offices

- Empowered country leadership

- Road shows and exhibitions

- Motorola weeks and days

- Office grand openings

- Key account management

- Focused advertising and public relations

- Cross-business teamwork

For the country, this simplifies contacts and relations since it offers a one-face-to-the-customer approach. For the company, it creates a higher awareness level externally and a better organizational efficiency internally.

The Emerging Market Development Fund. In 1988, the CEO created an Emerging Market Development Fund (EMDF) to promote rapid establishment of leadership positions in key emerging market areas. This program provides corporate assistance for a certain percentage of the cost for approved projects to encourage bolder and quicker development of these markets. (The EMDF is not a subsidy for normal business activities in these countries.) Projects for potential fund assistance are evaluated based upon the following criteria:

- Soundness of proposed project: Project consistency with business strategies, and its contribution to the goal of creating a leadership presence in the target market

- Extraordinary effort: The degree to which the project presents an effort which could not take place or would be significantly delayed if there was no EMDF assistance.

- Dedication of resources: The degree to which Motorola resources are dedicated to the targeted emerging market area.

The CEO emphasized the importance and benefits of the fund in an executive briefing. "We recognize that resources are limited, and these markets present a significant new challenge to us," he said. "Nevertheless, it is important to allocate appropriate time and resources to them. We must ensure that we support our existing customers who are, in some instances, leading the way into emerging markets. We must also set up our own most direct access to these very important regions. To speed market entry, the emerging market fund is a powerful tool."

The Tailwind of Aid Programs. Corporations were also able to apply for regional aid programs. These had been implemented by leading institutions and organizations, in recognition of the fact that the countries would not be strong enough to manage the transition process without support. The transfer of Western capital and know-how became two of the major driving forces. In the initial phase, their programs were not easily accessible because of the lack of information about the sources of such funds.

(A listing of Aid Programs can be found in the Appendix).

Added Value Programs. These are the lifeblood of the added value strategy. To make these initiatives available across the corporation, several knowledge-sharing platforms were created: a workshop, a worldwide database, training modules, case studies and Motorola publications.

In the two-day workshop based on an initiative of the Senior Executive Program (SEP), senior marketing, sales and distribution managers meet to:

- Exchange experiences and learn how to develop more effective value-added strategies to gain faster entry to new markets

- Apply the approach to current market entry activities

- Develop implementation plans

Figure 14 on the next page shows the objective, content and process elements of Knowledge Transfer.

Added-value programs enjoy one more distinct advantage; they do not necessarily require a big investment. As a matter of fact, the higher the added value, the lower the correlated relative investment will be. For instance, we may use the expertise of Turkey with leather goods to fabricate pocket cases for our radios. Such a relatively small investment will have high leverage in the region where this takes place, and the company will receive a high-quality accessory. (See Figure 15, Correlation between Strategy Intent and Materialization).

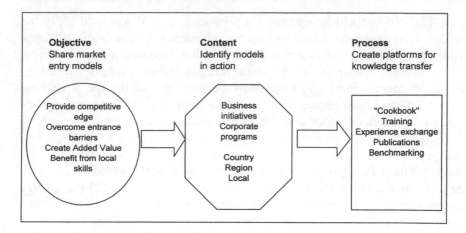

Figure 14: Knowledge Transfer

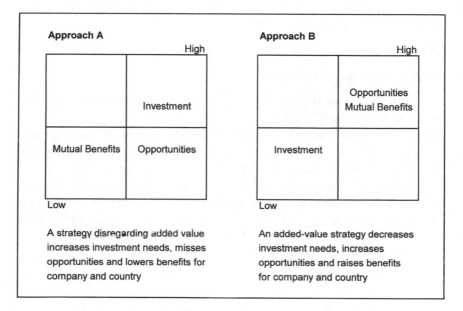

Figure 15: Correlation between Strategy Intent and Materialization

On the next pages there are samples of a wide range of added-value programs initiated by Motorola.

- **The Polish Supplier Initiative:** was jointly developed by Motorola and Warsaw University to select and qualify local companies as suppliers of new parts and communication goods.

- **The State Owned Enterprise Training Program - China:** This was developed by the Chinese State Department and Planning Commission and Motorola. The objective was to improve efficiency of state-owned enterprises and qualify them as potential suppliers.

- **The South Africa Black Dealer Program:** This aims at developing black enterprises and empowering previously disadvantaged people. Motorola, in turn, gains access to markets held by the black community.

- **The Rewrite School in South Africa:** This Motorola school, which is located in a township enables students to prepare for and take high school examinations.

- **The South Africa Education Fund:** This provides for the qualification of indigenous teachers in the subjects of mathematics and science at elementary schools.

- **Project HOPE in China:** This community program, organized by the Chinese Government, sponsors education of poor children in rural areas. Motorola provides donations, equipment and personal care. To date, numerous schools were built with Motorola funds.

- **China Accelerated Management Development Program (CAMP):** This program was designed to build a nucleus of a professional workforce. It is composed of classroom training, active learning, on the job training, job rotation in Motorola's worldwide facilities and project management.

- **Mission XXI:** An educational project involving 70 Latin American Universities. This is presented in more detail in Chapter 13.

- **Environment Protection in Costa Rica:** This joint program designed by the department for state education and Motorola is intended to improve awareness of future generations for environment protection. It is presented to 5th or 6th grade children from rural areas.

- **University Partnerships:** A large number of alliances, co-operations and joint ventures take place with leading colleges and universities. The main objective is to provide support in adjusting educational programs to future business and technological demands, to assist in the education of future professionals and managers, to promote scientific exchange and to enable access to talented students.

In response to the dramatic shortage of young talent in the early market entry phase, the following two programs were launched:

The European Talent Pool: This is a platform to recruit graduates from universities and colleges in emerging market countries based on specific business needs. The program provides a combination of practical work assignments and theoretical training within Western European businesses, and then reassigns the recruits to the job in the home country for which they had originally been identified.

The Cadre 2000 Plus: In order to meet the challenge of providing talented, high-potential candidates for leadership roles within Motorola's community worldwide, the multi-sector Cadre 2000 Plus training program has been established. Participants from Latin America, Europe, Middle East, Africa and the Asian Pacific region undergo a training program that includes:

- An intensive orientation to Motorola culture, values, goals and initiatives

- A US training program consisting of rotations in our major businesses

- Functional training in several key disciplines

- Regular training and debriefing sessions

- Final placement in the specific business and position in the candidate's country or region of origin

The Cadre 2000 Plus training structure enables Motorola to position multi-skilled, capable management candidates within growing markets. Graduates of this program carry both cultural and corporate awareness and experience into these global markets on all levels.

Both programs have been the backbone of a nucleus of young talent, many of whom now occupy leading positions. The programs are presently on hold but are intended to be re-activated once new needs arise.

The Motorola Foundation: The Motorola Foundation is legally separated from Motorola Inc. and operates under the United States Internal Revenue Service laws governing private foundations. Grants under this program have a charitable and non-profit status. They are designed to foster and support community and educational relations.

Projects intended for funding must meet certain eligibility criteria.

The United States Telecommunications Training Institute (USTTI):
The USTTI is a non-profit joint venture between leaders of the US communications industry and ranking officials from the federal government. The goal of this collaborative effort is to share the United States communications and technological advances on a global base. It also provides a comprehensive array of free telecommunications and broadcasting training courses for qualified women and men who manage the communication infrastructures in the developing countries of the world.

The Technical Assistance Program for the Commonwealth of Independent States (TACIS): This program was developed by the European Union for middle and senior managers from distributors, suppliers, customers, joint venture partners and associated companies. It acquaints them with our culture, organization, products, strategies and processes and provides the skills required to operate effectively in an open-market economy.

Training and Education: Training and education became an indispensable market-entry investment in light of the workforce's lack of knowledge and experience in business and management. Motorola University (MU) had a booth in our early road shows and was a permanent member in the emerging markets teams. MU designed and delivered a whole range of new programs and initiatives tailored to the specific needs of emerging markets. These covered leadership, business management, skills development, spectrum management, cultural diversity and many other topics. Without the sustained educational guidance and support our business would not have been able to fulfil their mission.

Often, demand was overwhelming. In China, Motorola tripled its workforce within five years to a five-digit number. New employees were mainly clerical, professional and managerial personnel. The company had to design a four-dimensional process: selection, coaching, training and retention. People were caught in between traditional management style, the legacy of the cultural revolution and the impositions of the 21st century. Most of them completely missed an entire development cycle that had taken place in the Western world over the past 30 years. And even retention became an early issue. The moment employees took over a key position they also became first class candidates for the rapidly growing competition.

The underlying training and qualification program was CAMP, previously described in this book.

How to Identify Possibilities for Added Value Programs. There are more opportunities than can be handled. It is the skill of management to pick the right programs to ensure maximum benefit and return on investment for both the country and the company. The strategic initiatives of developing countries for improving their performance are valuable resources. If these resources are handled with political correctness, tangible added value programs may be generated from that listing.

Strategic Initiatives for Further Progress most Common to Emerging Markets.

Political Arena	**Economic Arena**
Integrate into world community	Integrate into world economy
Stabilize democratization process	Liberalize legal framework
Develop reliable policy framework	De-regulate Key markets
Lead reforms	Improve investment climate
Remove boycotts	Upgrade Infrastructure
Fight terrorism and extremism	Increase local content
Reduce organized crime	Eliminate trade barriers
Abolish corruption	Create wealth

Social Arena	**Cultural Arena**
Improve education systems	Increase respect for cultural diversity
Reduce unemployment	Find a balance between tradition and modernism
Contain further urbanization	
Reduce gap between rich and poor	Create more liberal intellectual climate
Improve social welfare	
Fight against disease (Aids)	Share learning with other cultures
Abolish child labor	Implement affirmative action and equal employment

The New Dimension. The added value strategies described before convey a message: Any company doing business in emerging markets cannot succeed by itself, you need to take the local government, the workforce and your customers, suppliers, distributors and other business partners into your boat; to back up your investment by a sustained process of localization and added value creation. This particularly applies to the big booming economies like China, India, Russia and others. China's population is 4.5 times as big as in the US, and its economic performance is outgrowing the rest of the world.

In such huge markets, a company the following choices:

- Invest at low rate and you will position yourself as a low-profile operations

- Invest in niches and thus abandon plenty of other opportunities

- Invest on a large scale and become a local key player

Rick Younts (President of AP Regions) underlines what it takes to be successful:

"A global company cannot afford to miss business in these large markets. But a company cannot become a key player if it just imports into these markets. It needs investment in brick and mortar, manufacturing, distribution, R&D and, above all, people. Our investments in Asia are by far the biggest outside the US, but are commensurate to the needs and potential of these countries."

In this chapter the mutual benefits of added value strategies for the company of the country are highlighted. They are the door opener to market entry and underline our role as good citizen and premier employer. Furthermore, they economize investment needs and increase opportunities.

Chapter 9 - Field Experiences in Virgin Markets

Gaining Footholds in the Market Place

This chapter deals with the experiences collected by our Business Units in Central and Eastern Europe but also with other parts of the world where they started from a zero base. This was a scenario which no corporation and individual involved had ever faced before. These experiences may also serve as a recipe book for entering any future emerging markets where the initial conditions are expected to be similar.

The sequence of the described activities corresponds to the business rollout plan throughout the four-phase model. It does not reflect the organizational structure but the processes involved.

We have collected a large sample of functions so that the reader can derive maximum benefit for her or his own business.

Building Infrastructure in No Man's Land. The role of this business as a global provider of telecommunications infrastructures and network solutions was described in Chapter 2. This section covers the more operational aspects.

Klaus Rohn (Operations Director, Infrastructure Business, CEE) says the bottlenecks to market entry are always capacity and time. "We quickly recognized that the practice of bringing in a high number of expatriates and managing a project remotely was way too expensive and ineffective," Klaus says. "We reduced our core team to only a few Western experts and increased the number of local engineers, technicians and clerical personnel. We also outsourced parts of product development, material supply and installation work. Apart from some quality problems at the beginning, our experience with the education level, know-how and engagement of our partners and temporary employees was positive."

Cycle time was the second critical issue, according to Klaus. This mainly concerned rental contracts, construction permissions by local authorities and type approvals. His group faced unexpected difficulties and delays with local compliance and bureaucracy.

"The installation of local antenna sites turned out to be an adventure like in ancient pioneer times," he says. "Initially, we did not even find the location because we missed some turns in the road. We did not possess sufficient four-wheel-drive vehicles for the rough territory, and we had to use local students as translators to make ourselves understood to the local population."

Another challenge was the cooperation with well-established local telecommunications companies and Western joint-venture companies. "We had to accept our mutual weaknesses and build on our common strengths for the sake of joint success with the project," Klaus says. "And all the inconvenience and hard work were forgotten when we received thank-you letters like the one from a Hungarian citizen who had patiently waited 17 years for his phone connection."

Entrust Local Markets to Local People. The equipment business is divided up into various units comprising of design, manufacture, sale and servicing of wireless two way radio communications products and systems, systems solutions, related software and accessories to public and private customers.

Once frequency management, regulatory and type approval issues are resolved and the infrastructures are established, products, systems and services may be launched.

Axel Rettig (Director of Distribution, CEE / Central Asia, for a large business unit) became involved in the start-up. He and his team faced three major issues:

- Hiring and training the nucleus of the future local workforce.

- Building a dealer and distributor network.

- Establishing a central and local support infrastructure.

Axel found that there was no expertise and structure for the company's products and services. Still, the market potential and expectation level were enormous. This team was also positively surprised by the high education of its potential partners and employees.

"We rolled up our sleeves and just started," Axel says. "Our first discovery was the surprisingly low interest of our Western employees in an emerging market assignment at this time. We concentrated our hiring activities on young people working in one of our Western organizations but with local roots and vice versa; local citizens with either previous exposure to a Western company or employment in one of the state organizations involved in the radio communications field." This required a major training effort that forced Axel and his team to develop a complex training syllabus at an early stage. Looking back, this was fortunate because training became a competitive advantage for the company.

"The second task was to develop a network of strategic distribution partners," Axel says. "We looked for partners with an idea of our products, a vision about their and our future in the country, a commercial sense and a positive personal appearance." As compensation, Axel intended to give the partners market responsibility and develop them as entrepreneurs. He found many highly educated, motivated candidates who, over time, showed an unexpected level of loyalty and responsibility, and worked well together. Axel and his colleagues also established a set of rules for distributors and dealers to avoid overlapping interests and activities.

The third project was to establish a support structure to transfer as many functions as early as possible into the local markets to ensure close proximity to the customer, increase effectiveness and reduce the cost of remote Western support. "We achieved this gradually as soon as the countries reached a certain maturity and critical mass," Axel says. He is proud of some of his former trainees. Since then, a number of them who started a small garage business have become young entrepreneurs.

Double Your Time Frame and Halve Your Expections. Derek Phipps (Director of Distribution Systems Business, CEE) managed a business that served such customers as the Ministries of Interior and Defense; large state industries such as oil and gas; and state organizations like fire brigades, police and rescue services. This implies long-term relationships and opportunities for large orders. Consequently, his strategies needed to take into account circumstances that differed from those of short-term product sales.

Derek believes emerging markets follow other rules than mature ones. "There are major paradigm shifts that require us to forget some of our previous experience," Derek says. "One of our first observations was that whatever sales you plan for your business, you have to cut it by 50 percent and add two more years."

In the first year of entering an emerging country, it is critical to understand that market in its totality. We do this with the aid of our worldwide Opportunity Data Base, which allows a close look at market potential, key opportunities, potential customer base, infrastructure and technology requirements, and other key issues. "This market intelligence is used to develop an investment and prioritization pattern," Derek says.

It is usually only in the second year of market entry that some of the identified sales opportunities start to materialize. This process will only be successful if it is backed up by sustained support in the areas of infrastructure development, consulting, training and financing solutions, according to Derek. During this stage, it is wise to watch the market carefully to record and interpret the key messages and to identify any concerns that may cause delays.

Business Development Needs Creativity. This semiconductor business (since 2004 an independent legal entity) is a leading provider of embedded processors, which offer multiple technologies and solutions for smart products in many industrial fields. To gain a foothold in the emerging markets up-front involvement and patience are required. Uwe v. Ammon (Business Development Manager Semiconductor Business, CEE) describes a scenario which is typical for former command economies where the electrical and electronics industries have been over-proportionally badly affected by the economic changes. According to Uwe "...this left us with two choices: to turn on our heels or to make a long-term investment. Whenever systems fall apart, the alternative is to address the people, because they survive the systems," Uwe continues. "In our case, the ideal target group was the universities. The first strategy was to donate development systems for micro-controllers, microprocessors and digital signaling processors to leading universities so that students could become familiar with our company and learn to work with our products.

The second strategy was to enable professors with university chairs to acquire state-of-the-art knowledge, allowing Motorola to benefit from their important role in science and industry."

Uwe states the third strategy aimed at providing added value programs in cooperation with the universities. Here are some common activities:

- Providing assistance to qualify for a financial aid program

- Pooling companies with a certain technical development need together with the right resources

- Developing an educational program for design engineers together with a local university

- Outsourcing engineering projects, thus capitalizing on local expertise and creating employment

- Involving universities in training and upgrading local dealers and distributors

- Using a country more advanced in a certain technology as a model for less progressed ones

"Western corporations with local subsidiaries in the electrical and electronic fields are in desperate need of local technical advice and support on the basis of Western know-how," says Uwe. "Our early presence and extensive infrastructure became a lever for qualifying us in this role and for following our Western customers into their new local markets."

This long-term strategy required staying power, patience and a high degree of persuasiveness even within our own company. "We are still not where we wish to be, but our increasing sales numbers are proof of the validity of our concept," Uwe confirms. "It is supported by the slow but steady recovery of local industry, especially in the PC and white goods markets. Everything was there before but used in a different direction, disregarding productivity, quality, customers and competition. In this process emerging markets can build on their rich industrial history and large intellectual resources."

We Are with You. A well-structured rollout plan, ongoing relationship building and long-term customer commitment are the ingredients of a successful distribution strategy.

Jeff Spaeth (General Manager, for a large business unit, LAC) describes the way in which this business was established in Latin America. This process closely followed the pathway described in figure 16.

"In the 70's and 80's our sector exported our upper range of two-way radios to commercial, government and industrial customers in Latin America through local distributors and dealers. Like many US corporations we used Miami as our regional hub and traveled in and out. We also worked with Miami based exporters to assist with the initial sales of products into the region.

After this initial period of 'market seeding' and the launch of a product line designed for low and medium incomes in the 90's we started to establish our local presence. In view of the large territory to be covered we applied the beachhead concept by combining mutually accessible countries that agreed to this arrangement under one head office, e.g. Argentina together with Chile and Columbia with Venezuela. To the extent we built and expanded our local teams we reduced the expatriate staff.

In the third phase, the sector installed local marketing expertise and support functions, thus moving away from the central support out of the US. Over time, other operations such as manufacturing in Brazil followed. The entire market entry process was coordinated with the rolling in of other Motorola businesses to ensure a unified approach.

By means of a structured and sustained market entry process in Latin America our sector changed from an export organization to a strong local supplier dedicated to this exciting part of the world."

Throughout the past two decades in Latin America, Motorola has been challenged by the "roller coaster" effects of the individual economies and the frequent change in political leadership on the stability of the region.

Although this aggravated the consistency of our activities we made it our policy not to react to these ups and downs but to continually maintain a local presence level. Jeff Spaeth points out how his business unit endorsed this policy during a specific event:

"The message to our dealers during the Mexico Tequila crisis in the mid 90's was, "We are with you!" Several years later the audience of a dealer convention returned the same statement to Motorola. Our commitment in tough times paid off in terms of the loyalty shown us by our local partners later."

Sales Are Strategic. "Emerging markets are poised for a rapid uptake." Eike Bär says. "There is an enormous backlog and potential. In the years to come, they will be a major contributor to our business growth and even bypass some of our traditional Western markets.

To participate in the perspectives, however, we need to understand the forces that drive our customers and surround the sales target," Eike continues. "Increasingly, decisions are based on political and strategic interests rather than on pure technical and commercial data. It is, therefore, not good enough to just work with our product portfolio, we should also acquaint ourselves with our partners' matrix organization, the power distribution and their agenda. Based on these insights it is important to find out the common denominators and use them as a starting point.

In the case of large strategic business, decisions may not even be in the hands of the customer but could be met at a country level. This frequently happens in the case of projects with the ministries of interior and defense. Occasionally, a major external event, such as governmental elections, interrupts the process and we are faced with a new scenario.

Cultural diversity is another dimension. Dealing in different cultural environments required a fine-tuning of our approach. In the South Eastern Hemisphere trust and personal ties played a predominant role. One had to conduct business in person and ensure continuity of relations. We frequently found ourselves in a situation where we could not determine the final decision takers but usually only met the last but one."

Here are some of the areas of interest that may influence business decisions:

- **The Customer**
  Get state of the art products and services
  Receive financial aid/support
  Strengthen strategic position
  Share Western know-how
  Upgrade own infrastructure

- **The Supplier**
  Gain access to local market
  Generate business
  Become regional player
  Strengthen geo-strategic position
  Be ahead of competition
  Benefit from local know-how

Survival. With this subject, we enter the higher ranks of politics and diplomacy. Often, this represents a predominant common interest of two partners within a global scenario. To the outside world, relevant activities may be camouflaged as regional development programs, but there is much more behind the nice package.

At a country and regional level it is frequently in the vital interest of governments to help a political system survive for the sake of self-protection. Russia, for example, was on an intravenous drip of Western financial aid for many years to prevent a relapse into the old systems, which would have been a tragedy for the entire world. Similar situations are found all over: in Latin America, the Middle East and Central Africa. The concept of most military and financial aid programs is based on survival strategies.

Often, such programs are coupled with the latent economic interest of the other side, and the wolf appears in sheep's clothing. To the extent Western markets become increasingly saturated, emerging markets are an outlet for stagnation in the home market and create new demand. At the beginning of the 90's, many Western countries were in a recession mode, resulting in economic stimulation for investment and consumer goods in the new markets.

Consumer Behavior – Pure Psychology. In order to make the right decisions in our business in the public and private sectors, it is important to understand the needs and behavior of our end users. Here is a summary of our observations.

In command economies goods were produced according to a plan, which was subordinate to government needs and disregarded the role of consumers. Moreover, the plan neglected seasonal conditions, so it was often that gloves could be seen in the stores in summer and sunshades in winter.

In the first cycle directly after the fall of communism in Europe it was only natural that the people satisfied the repressed needs of former years in buying clothing, household goods and foodstuff. When the years of product shortage and monotony were over they were hungry for state of the art products and high quality brand names. Domestic products were neglected because the new lifestyle dictated that the breakfast table was decked with Irish butter and English jam. This period was typified by emotional consumer behavior.

One area of particular interest was the procurement of a telephone. This was seen as synonymous to access to the new free world. Therefore, the telephone business experienced a tremendous boom and telephone companies had a difficult time getting the lines installed on time.

The second cycle dealt with the fulfillment of dreams, which could not have been realized before, for example a two-week vacation on a Caribbean beach, a new car or a stereo system. (Before, only a few standard car models were available. A sports car was seen as a car with a pair of tennis shoes in the trunk!) During this cycle many people tended to overspend.

In the third cycle we observed user planned spending e.g. for a house renovation or a larger apartment. Consumers also started to invest in savings plans. It was in this phase that people generally returned to their domestic products. They realized that Irish butter was more expensive and not much better than the butter from the local cow. This was the time when local production, supported by the West, picked up in terms of product variety and quality.

Such patterns of consumer behavior are also found in many other emerging markets.

A Defect 500 Miles Away. At the same time as the market set-up of various business activities takes place, aftermarket operations are being established. Armin Hanus (Director Aftermarket Operations, EMEA) presents the challenges and obstacles of this activity in developing countries.

"Motorola's aftermarket operations are composed of service (maintenance and repair), parts supply and accessory sales. The key success factors are best-in-class cycle time, premier quality and close customer relations. In the Western world this means, for instance, that 90 percent of customer parts and accessory orders are shipped on the day the order is received and are usually in the customer's hands on the next day. With respect to service, defective radios are repaired on the day of receipt and returned by night courier to the closest hub so that the radio arrives at the customer site within 48 hours of the initial contact. Unfortunately, this fastidious process does not work in the emerging markets for a variety of reasons.

Although we manage to ensure that the requested parts or accessories and the repaired radios arrive at the port of entry within two days, our eager objectives are frequently jeopardized by complicated customs and import regulations, an exorbitant bureaucracy and a high loss risk. In spite of minimizing transportation risks by selecting Western or reliable local shipping companies, the ratio of lost product, as compared to the Western world, is approximately 10 to 1. Often, last minute surprises further aggravate the situation. For example, Russia now demands that all paperwork be produced in the native language.

To overcome these barriers and, at the same time, improve our relationship with customers in the country, we are establishing regional repair centers to serve as local hubs. Depending on our strategic intent and the legal framework of the country, these centers may be created in the form of a partnership, a joint venture or a stand-alone operation. In remote areas, we may also use a local distributor.

Local presence often presents a dilemma in itself because it raises the expectation of high local employment. We have to make our partners understand that the benefit of local presence is not large employment, but rather the creation of a whole added-value chain.

Another complication is domestic transportation within large territories. In the absence of fast and reliable long-distance connections, radios, parts and accessories are frequently hand-carried."

In countries like Russia, where the former system had generated a high degree of improvisation, local technicians tended to repair radios by themselves rather than exchanging parts and modules. In other regions, such as Black Africa, we were faced with a different view of maintenance and repair. Maintaining the quality and function of radios through regular care was not always a priority of the local staff. Radios were used as long as they work and then cannibalized or thrown away.

"The yardstick for quality varies by region," Armin continues. "We face different perceptions of products and service quality not only with our own staff. Often a customer does not recognize our quality and customer satisfaction efforts and is not willing to pay for more than he or she wants or needs. It will be a future challenge to convince our customers that with our quality and total customer satisfaction standards, they will gain a competitive advantage toward their own customers."

From Garage Assembly to Manufacturing Excellence. Manufacturing in most emerging markets originates from their culture of craftsmanship and small garage assembly. Educational programs were not geared to modern manufacturing processes and industrial engineering. The first generation of manufacturing facilities was designed for badge production with mechanical assembly lines. In Asia it was the Japanese, who introduced quality and cycle time as competitive advantages. On the human resource side the traditional hierarchical structures hampered flexibility and creativity.

In the Middle East and Africa the low industrial base did not breed a manufacturing culture. In Central and Eastern Europe the command economy destroyed old manufacturing traditions such as were present in the Czech Republic, which was recognized as a high quality manufacturing producer before World War II. The communist regime installed a production mentality disregarding any productivity issues. The breakdown of the system was, to a large extent, a consequence of their lack of response to global competition.

A memorable turnaround was achieved in Asia where we now find a high degree of manufacturing excellence. Many of the production plants have become international benchmarks, and China is becoming the "factory of the world".

In the meantime, Motorola operates large feeder plants as part of global supply chain management in China, Malaysia and Singapore but also in other regions such as Mexico, to name only a few.

At the same time market factories are required to gain a foothold in critical local markets. Prior to planning in such an operation, some critical issues need attention:

- The market focus may not be in line with critical mass and productivity needs.

- Our own factory management must be convinced that no tangible return on investment might be realized.

- The local management must understand that the primary goal is not large-scale production and mass employment but the distribution outlet.

One of our product groups wanted to establish an operation providing access to public safety market segments. We worked with a local company in Eastern Europe, which achieved all the necessary parameters in terms of quality, cycle time and productivity. Even so the cooperation between them did not work out as expected. Both sides had overestimated the distribution capabilities.

Another company was formed in Central Asia with the participation of a local distributor and a state owned company. This was successful because the distributor disposed of the distribution networks and the state owned company opened the door to local government and decision-makers.

These two cases underline the importance of a good up-front strategy.

New Partnerships Through Local Sourcing. Local Sourcing is a component of supply chain management and added value strategy. In many countries, local sourcing is a local content requirement. Emerging markets offer many advantages in view of their untapped resources, solid technical skills and favorable commercial conditions. Especially in the Asian countries the many family type businesses with their traditional craftsmanship background provide abundant opportunities.

It's a win-win scenario. The local suppliers benefit from the company's know-how, receive extensive training and support and may acquire official qualifications. The company, in turn, establishes a supplier base in support of its local operations and can learn from unusual but successful skill applications. Often, locally provided components are re-exported to serve global markets.

In China, Motorola started partnerships with promising domestic suppliers as early as 1992. This is part of the company's strategy to equip each investment with a localization plan aimed at working with local suppliers and helping them to meet qualifications and efficiency standards.

In the meantime quite a few of the local suppliers have acquired Total Customer Satisfaction Awards and official recognition. They have opened up their own businesses and are capable themselves of serving local and export markets. The company, in turn, has achieved a local content of over 60% generated by a three-digit number of qualified suppliers.

For the Motorola experts involved in this project it was a unique learning experience about other cultures, the abundant potential inherent in our emerging markets and the enrichment of working together with wonderful people.

Uncut Diamonds: The R&D Potential. Dr. Robert C. Pfahl (Director International and Environmental R&D) describes the challenging processes and networking applied in establishing local R&D and the mutual benefits of such an initiative for the emerging markets and the corporation involved.

"In 1994 Motorola decided to globalize their Advanced Technology R&D activities. The first R&D center, founded in Europe in Wiesbaden, Germany, was followed by two centers for emerging markets. The second R&D center in Beijing/Tianjin, China, opened the following year. The approach used in Germany became the prototype in establishing other centers. There were three objectives in creating these labs:

1. Global access to the best advanced technology R&D and infrastructure

2. Acquiring technology in technical areas which could benefit the organization

3. Supporting Motorola's regional engineering and manufacturing operations

The expected benefits to Motorola were to:

1. Reduce cycle time for implementing new technology

2. Acquire superior and critical technology such as Product Simulation

3. Reduce R&D and implementation costs

Advanced Technology R&D identifies, develops and implements technology related to designing and manufacturing products: particularly electronic packaging, manufacturing processing, electronic materials, optimization and advanced components. After the formation of the initial center in Germany it became clear that the emerging markets of Eastern Europe possessed a strong, differentiated research base that could serve as the foundation for additional development activities. Strong on-going research relationships have been developed with the University of Wroclaw, Poland and the University of Mining and Metallurgy in Krakau, Poland. The research in Krakau has focused on manufacturing optimization and environmental materials research, and the developed technology has been transferred to Motorolans globally. In addition Motorola Labs Global Software Group has been able to establish a software-center in Krakau because of their excellent intellectual resources.

The original selection of Wiesbaden in Germany as the first site was based upon its strong manufacturing research base, the location of the Motorola infrastructure and ease of transportation. In this case key elements in establishing a successful organization were identifying the Country Manager as the strong local Motorola champion for the center, receiving strong support from the Director of Human Resources and other critical infrastructure providers and performing an extensive benchmarking of the regional R&D infrastructure. Additionally from that base it was essential to select a well-recognized and networked individual to lead the organization.

The Asian research center in China was our first major center established in an emerging market. For the most part the successful model established in Germany was used. Here too, Motorola's Country President was a strong champion for establishing the center. In the case of China, however, the goal was to fund much of the activity from the regional businesses since the emphasis would be more to support local companies. Developing an equitable funding model took a great deal of negotiating with the businesses, but this activity was supported strongly by the China Controller, who recognized the ultimate financial benefit to the organization. The Chinese academic community, Science and Technology Ministry and the Chinese Academy of Science were more than willing to meet and discuss their R&D, but initially it was hard to judge the strength of these activities. At first, in spite of strong support from the HR organization, it was also difficult to identify a local individual who could become the leader of the organization and individual researchers. Therefore, for the first years we used expatriates to lead the China Center until we could identify and develop a local leader.

In identifying and developing our external research partners in China we took advantage of international conferences and the expertise of professors with whom we were already doing research in Europe. In many cases the European professors had established partnerships with Chinese universities and were cross-training Chinese graduate students at their universities. We built ties to these Chinese universities and professors and started offering internships to their students to identify and develop our own researchers. Initially, we established the lab in Beijing because of the excellent transportation and outstanding research institutes. We soon realized, however, that it was more important to locate the center in Tianjin at our manufacturing site so that the young researchers could benefit from daily contact with manufacturing operations.

At present the Chinese lab is under local leadership and the staff conducts R&D projects that benefit Motorola globally. The joint research between the Motorola staff and Chinese institutions has been published in well-respected international journals and presented at major international conferences.

A third centre was operating in Brazil. Learning from our China experience we had initially co-located the centre with Motorola's major manufacturing site. The local supporter for this center was the General Manager of the plant. The funding model had been to use local R&D tax incentive funds. Again, strong ties had been established to the Director of Human Resources and we had benchmarked the local R&D infrastructure. We had learned that there were several excellent R&D universities as well as an established pool of researchers in the Campinas region of Sao Paulo State because of other multinational companies that had come and gone during the previous decade. Again, we had built bridges to universities and professors who were connected to the international R&D community.

A number of benefits from these activities have been reaped. By establishing environmental R&D programs in China, Poland and Brazil in conjunction with our main activities in Germany and the United States we have learned that our research into proactive environmental technology in emerging markets is synergistic with Motorola's other activities. Each of the emerging markets faces unique needs and offers opportunities for the environment. Motorola always meets or exceeds the international standards in all of their global activities. Our regional environmental programs have allowed us to work with local suppliers to help them achieve international standards, to assist government groups and aid other manufacturing firms to become proactive. This effort has enabled us to create strong local environmental university programs that have trained competent research-ers.

In summary, research results support the realization of the expected benefits. The projects have added value not only to the emerging markets but also to the company as a whole. Co-locating R&D operations with manufacturing operations in an emerging market has made the business 'whole' while allowing us to address local product and business issues lo-cally."

Dr. Yefim Bukhman (Director Semiconductor Technology Planning, EMEA) presents a business case that highlights the benefits of long term planning and up-front investment within the semiconductor products sec-tor.

"Inspired by several factory visits in Russia and the excellent work of some Russian professors at the Russian Academy of Sciences, the semi-conductor general management sent me to Russia in 1993 to prepare the ground for local R&D," Jeff says. "I conducted interviews with Russian scientists who emerged from the former Academy of Sciences and had founded their own small enterprises in Moscow and St. Petersburg. They were affected by the withdrawal of government funding, and our offer of subcontracting them came just in time."

But, Jeff points out that there were some in-built inconveniences. "We could not ensure that they were working exclusively for Motorola," he says. "The protection of our intellectual property rights was at potential risk, and the loyalty and dedication was not as strong as under our own employment. It was therefore a logical decision to establish our own R&D organization." Jeff describes the benefits of this decision: "We inherited a group of extremely well-educated, skilled and dedicated professionals. It required a major up-front investment into language and technology train-ing, especially in software development, and into managing the mental change from theoretical to applied research. In return, we received an in-creasing number of patent applications and were able to increase our staff for our global R&D activities. This more than offsets the high bureaucratic hurdles that we found at the beginning."

In this chapter we have shared the experiences collected by specific business leaders in a virgin market environment. They were faced with a multitude of problems but rewarded by numerous opportunities. The strong impact of culture was recognized early on and much was learnt as a consequence. The critical success factor lies in viewing the problems as a challenge and not seeing the challenge as a problem.

Chapter 10 - The Crucial Role of Corporate Functions

Supporting the Local Business

Contrary to business reports, which are related to specific markets and applicable to the individual segments of the four-phase model, corporate support is indispensable throughout all phases.

Starting from a Zero Baseline. The Government Relations activities include all regulatory, frequency management and type approval activities. They are in the front line of market entry to pave the way for our telecommunications business and to anticipate the length of time needed for type approvals.

H.C. Heng (Director Government Relations and Standards, EMEA) reports that in the initial start-up phase in the Middle East and Africa telecommunications were generally far behind the Western world in terms of regulatory structure and service. Most countries had no frequency management and type approval process in place. "We also had to keep in mind that government officials did not necessarily share our perceptions and goals," H.C says. "It was therefore important to respect their specific needs and build up personal trust and fruitful relations."

Herbert Erd (Manager Government Relations and Telecommunications, CEE) describes the various steps involved in installing a telecommunications type approval infrastructure.

The first task was to identify those ministries and government agencies responsible for the regulatory framework, to analyze their organizational structure and to determine the experts and decision-makers. Highly qualified engineers who were technology-oriented but did not understand business occupied the ministries. Consequently, projects submitted to them for evaluation were assessed by their technical, not commercial, potential. Also, each ministry carried responsibility for a subordinated industry so that decisions always were, and still are, weighted in light of their positive or negative effect on that industry.

All countries belonging to the former communist system worked with similar frequencies and spectrum allocations to military, security and TV, but very limited to mobile services. "We only identified a few available low-band and mid-band frequencies for which we had no adequate products," Herbert says. "Frequency management was once a military domain and is slowly becoming liberalized. This results in extensive cycle times ranging from three months to three years."

All products sold must be type-approved and quality-certified. "The process is somewhat strenuous but it works," Herbert continues. "Quality certification was performed by ISO 9000. Since there was no related experience in dealing with this standard, each ministry designed its own version. Certification was further aggravated by the lack of accredited ISO specialists in emerging markets. A mutual recognition of type approval and quality certification standards is on the wish list of both sides, but will still take some time."

"It is a challenging task to hire local government relations professionals to execute these sensitive tasks," Herbert says. "The profile calls for expertise in government and regulatory work, previous exposure to Western companies, high engineering and management capabilities and diplomatic skills. Candidates must be young enough to not be influenced by the old school but old enough to be accepted by authorities. And they must be knowledgeable about the regulatory environment," he adds.

Herbert says he had good experiences with candidates from the former academies of science, the foreign relations departments of governments and the ministries of defense.

Motorola supports this process with spectrum management and type approval seminars for government officials to help them brush up on their telecommunications policy and infrastructure. Such support also includes special projects such as a frequency allocation inventory in Bangladesh jointly performed with their university of engineering and technology.

A Roll-Out Plan for Finance. The finance organization is in charge of setting up the commercial and financial policies and procedures relevant to conducting business in the emerging markets. It is also the custodian of Motorola's standards of internal control to ensure compliance with internal and external regulations and laws.

Karlheinz Ullius (Director Corporate Finance Germany, CEE) describes the key issues and activities in this process:
"It is the responsibility of finance to designate the type of local structure needed to meet the business purpose and adjust this to changing requirements. While in some countries a representative office may be adequate, a different set of local activities might require a permanent structure, such as a subsidiary. The legal structure also determines the type and extent of financial services in the country ranging from remote support in the embry-

onic stage of a local presence to a complete finance department in a mature organization.

Developing and implementing financial policies and procedures is another priority. They have to fulfill three purposes: fully correspond to the overriding Motorola policies and procedures, be in compliance with local legislation and practices, and present a working tool for local finance staff. In our case it was not easy to reconcile these conflicting requirements. In a major effort, we prepared a handbook including detailed operating instructions and forms. We emphasized our code of conduct and standards of internal control, and trained our local employees on these policies.

During the first years, local banks were not yet prepared for non-cash payment. Local bills had to be paid via petty cash, which included salaries, company cars, furniture, import duties and local services. Cash was only changed into local currency at the time of payment to minimize exchange rate losses. This exposed our finance people to high risk since they had to travel around with suitcases full of money.

In an attempt to accompany the corporation's move into emerging markets with a meaningful information tool, finance developed a business information system. This reflects business and country's sales by month in actual and year-to-date numbers with quarterly and annual forecasts. The system also reports budget performance.

In consideration of the complex interaction and workflow between the central and local finance organization, we appointed an experienced accounting professional in our home office to act as the coordination point. This position is an indispensable investment that allows us to use our local secretaries to perform the basic finance and accounting tasks in the early stages, prior to accountants coming on board."

"The day-to-day operations are still exposed to a range of inconveniences," says Steve Herne (Director Corporate Finance, CEE). One bureaucratic hurdle is trying to understand local compliance. Laws are always changing, so it is difficult to know which laws presently apply. "Even as more laws are following the Western model, tax offices deliberately or unconsciously still use the old laws," Steve says. "Regions work on the principle of form over substance coupled with unacceptable paperwork and requirements. Companies that do not comply risk high fines regardless of evidence of correctness. This is particularly critical in the areas of custom duty, import and export business, and added-value tax." Other problems are old accounting methods not permitting accruals, four to eight times more accounting lines than in the West and awkward legal systems.

"Our supreme principle is therefore to fully comply with all local financial laws and requirements whether they make sense or not, and oblige our employees to their strict adherence," Steve says. "This stringent policy has paid off since, in some countries, we were able to become the benchmark for other Western corporations and local administrations."

Quite a number of our customers are determined to buy our state of the arts products, systems and service but they have only a limited financial capability. David Small (Director Corporate Finance, EMEA) comments, "To address this issue the European Management Board has endorsed a key initiative which is to develop customer financing as an intelligent solution and a core competency. The ultimate goal was to design package proposals combining a technical solution with a financing plan. We developed a training course composed of modules tailored to specific business needs. It was done in close co-operation with leading international banks and financial corporations. We also encouraged our business to employ trade finance experts in their organizations to work together with the technical experts. We experienced a mutual learning process; our finance people became more knowledgeable about the business and the business people recognized the importance of trade financing for their success. The program was also used in Latin America and Asia, another example of global learning and know-how transfer."

Compliance in an Arbitrary Environment. Prior to market entry it is the Law Department's responsibility to investigate the local legislative framework and to establish the legal base for business activities. The Law Department is also the custodian of our Code of Conduct and corporate governance programs to ensure compliance with internal and external business ethics. During the process our lawyers analyzed and sought to emphasize some of the "red flag" cases that needed particular attention in order to avoid risks or pitfalls. The list is not elaborative and merely intended to raise awareness.

Legislation in many emerging markets is still subject to rapid change. Frequently, room for interpretation is left, which may be exploited by the local authorities in favor of the domestic market partner. Western corporations have a hard time keeping track and risk high fines, even if they can prove that compliance was not violated or was not achieved due to the error of another party.

In Russia new laws that are passed are not only valid from the date they are passed but are also frequently retrospectively effective. This may mean additional obligations. In China commentaries, operating procedures and court rulings, which are important for legal decisions are, in general, not disclosed, which often leaves foreign companies in the dark. Jurisdiction processes are lengthy and complicated, while law enforcement and a sense of justice become less important the further the distance to the business center.

There are a number of countries, which are excluded from business because Western countries and/or corporations are on their boycott list. Such boycotts are also applied in the opposite direction.

The US Government has issued a Commerce Control List as part of their Export Administration Regulations. It applies to those technologies requiring an export license before they can be exported. Such licenses do not only pertain to products but also to people. Local employees hired from certain countries need to be granted a license to allow them to work in sensitive technology areas as specified by the US Bureau of Export Administration. Other governments enforce similar procedures.

In some Middle East regions, such as the United Arab Emirates, commercial activities are not allowed without an officially appointed and registered sponsor or agent, normally a high level local national or reputed local company. The law regulates duties and responsibilities. Alongside the general service provided, sponsorship is indispensable for business promotion.

How to Protect and Generate Intellectual Property. Dr. Robert Handy (Director Intellectual Property Rights, EMEA) addresses one of the most burning issues of any corporation, namely how to protect its intellectual property rights in the emerging markets. He highlights not only the legal and technical aspects, but also the historical and social backgrounds.

"Under the old system of the command economies, the creators of intellectual property were recognized and perhaps even rewarded by receiving a promotion or a better standard of living, but the government was the proprietor of the intellectual property rights. This meant that the government controlled the exploitation of the intellectual property and kept most of the economic benefit. Inventions, works or trademarks created outside the country were usually treated differently than those created by local citizenry. To the extent permitted by treaty, these 'foreign' creations could be registered and their intellectual property rights nominally owned and controlled by the foreign entity or a domestic agent of the foreign entity. But, as a practical matter, the communist governments did whatever they wanted; private ownership of intellectual property and intellectual property rights was effectively absent from these countries.

Under command economies the idea of private ownership of intellectual property and intellectual property rights is less than ten years old. Under the old system people were led to believe by their governments that ideas, inventions, software, etc., could be freely used by anyone - they belonged to the state for the betterment of all. People believed this for the better part of their lives. A cultural consequence of this era has been that most of the citizens of these countries think differently about intellectual property than people in the West do.

Another important cultural value has been the lack of reliance on the civil courts to settle disputes. For more than a thousand years the idea of a body of rules independent of the sovereign, to which even the sovereign must conform, did not exist in command economies. Hence, it should be no surprise that ordinary citizens and business people do not think of a court as a vehicle to resolve disputes. In the past, they could never be sure of an impartial hearing."

With the collapse of the former systems most countries rushed to modernize their intellectual property laws. Without a modern set of intellectual property laws, Western companies were reluctant to bring new technology into the area. English translations of the intellectual property laws are available from the World Intellectual Property Office (WIPO) in The Hague.

In summary, it can be stated that a legal framework is in place but often lacks enforcement.

Trademark piracy and blackmail have become a significant industry where Western consumer goods companies enter developing countries for the first time. In many countries, a trademark is effectively obtained by registration rather than use and is granted to the entity that first registers it in that country, without regard to whether or not it is a well known trade label outside the country.

Counterfeit goods are rampant in many emerging market countries. They appear anywhere there is significant demand and available cash. Much of this activity takes place on the black market, which means they avoid some or all of the business transaction taxes.

Most of the knock-off goods come from the Far East and China where they are manufactured cheaply, sometimes under the protection of their governments. They carry the trademarks of famous brands and are in many cases at a casual glance indistinguishable from the original, even though not of the same quality. Because the practice is carried out by a comparatively large number of small importer-sellers, it requires constant vigilance and enforcement by the trademark owner in his own market to protect his product. If the trademark owner gathers evidence and presents a good case, the local police will usually help the trademark owner seize the counterfeit goods.

Gray market or parallel imports refer to importation and sale of real products of the trademark owner (not counterfeits) into a country where some other local firm has the exclusive right to sell such products (e.g., the trademark owner's officially authorized local distributor). The gray market importer buys his product directly or indirectly from the trademark owner outside the country in question, then imports it in parallel to the authorized distributor and sets it up in competition to the authorized distributor.

In some countries, the trademark owner or the distributor, who has the exclusive right to use the trademark, can stop the gray market parallel imports by a court action and by working with the customs service. In other countries, the exhaustion rule applies and the parallel gray market imports cannot be stopped. The exhaustion rule says that the trademark owner's rights are exhausted once the product has been placed in commerce somewhere, and the owner cannot prevent the gray market importer from bringing it into the territory of the distributor. Under these circumstances, the only recourse is to shut off the gray market importer's supply of the goods by preventing him or her from buying them elsewhere. This is often very hard to do.

When a new company, domestic or foreign, wishes to start business it must pick a name that is unique. The name cannot conflict with or be confusingly similar to the name of another company in the same or a similar line of business. This is basic commercial law. Unfortunately, in many countries this can be very difficult because of a lack of a central registry and/or computerized records of business names. The search must usually be done by hand from paper records in a lot of places. Where the trade name is also intended to serve as a trademark, this can be a significant problem.

While the risks of losing control over intellectual property in these countries is certainly greater than in typical Western countries, it is not insurmountable. It is part of the overall evaluation of the business risk that is involved in entering a new market. Considering a number of basic issues discussed below can substantially reduce the risk.

- Emphasize physical security and training in the handling and retention of proprietary information. It is much better to limit distribution of, or access to confidential information than to rely on contractual obligations against disclosure.

- Assume that the government intelligence services will have access to any proprietary information you bring into the country or develop there, and evaluate how the business risk from that can be controlled (i.e., what is the government likely to do with the information). You may be better off developing a cordial relationship with the local intelligence service than trying to prevent their penetrating your organization.

- It is probably more important to spend time evaluating the character of prospective local business partners you are dealing with than agonizing over the detailed wording of the intellectual property license or commercial contract you are about to sign. American firms in particular too often present long US-style contracts. These complex legal documents are the result of studying a hundred years of English and American court decisions interpreting the law and the language of past contracts. They attempt to cover every eventuality and possibility. But it is a mistake to rely on them in foreign countries to enforce what you think are the contract terms in the same way that you might in the US for several reasons:

1. The other party will probably not understand the document in the same way you do, especially if it is English.

2. In these countries, contracts are often not viewed with the same degree of reverence that we expect in the West. Contracts are often just the starting point of the relationship, not the defining document. Remember that they did not grow up on "rule of law" as a sacred mantra.

3. Lower court judges will probably not understand a complex document. If they cannot understand it, you are not going to get the enforcement you expect.

4. In these countries, the most important aspect of a successful deal is usually the personal relationship you develop with the other party.

The new intellectual property laws that have been enacted in these countries theoretically provide similar protection to what is found in the West, albeit with some gaps and anomalies. But usually, litigation history is lacking so you cannot tell in advance how the local courts will interpret the law when you want to enforce your intellectual property rights. That is why when you are drafting an agreement to be enforced in such courts you make sure that the agreement is simple and clear. Make the judge's job as easy as you can.

Avoid future disputes by carefully doing your homework in advance, understanding that the other party may be motivated by a completely different set of values than you. For example, if you are negotiating a technology deal with a former communist apparatchik, do not expect him to have the same agenda as you do. In his frame of reference, a successful deal may be a personal negative.

Dealing with intellectual property issues in these countries involves challenges and opportunities. Great opportunities exist to create new intellectual property and use the fruits of intellectual property that have already been created. Do not be intimidated by the process of securing intellectual property rights. The potential rewards outweigh the risks.

Communications in a Changing Environment. In the early days of emerging market entry, communications were hampered or even endangered by bureaucratic hurdles, and the lack of adequate communication tools, professional individuals, agencies and media, which were not used to the Western style of communications. These adverse conditions have rapidly and substantially improved, as Shelagh Lester-Smith (Vice President Corporate Communications and Public Affairs) points out.

"Communicating in emerging markets continues to be challenging, though technology has helped overcome some of the problems we would have encountered as we entered emerging markets ten years ago.

Today, we can expect to exchange and share information with the media and other key constituents via computer, for example, in most of our emerging markets. Today, we can invite press to a Motorola event by fax or by e-mail, and in most emerging markets where we do business today; the postal service has grown in efficiency by leaps and bounds.

The very notion of public and media relations has evolved considerably in emerging markets, with the growth of local boutique agencies on the one hand and the establishment of international/global full service communications consultancies on the other. Typically staffed with energetic and talented young people, they bring a wide range of possibilities to the markets, and create important links for clients with other in country constituents, as well as being able in many cases to speak English, still the lingua franca of the communications industry.

The media too have evolved in their markets. Today, most emerging countries boast cable and satellite broadcast possibilities; the print media has been rationalized and cleaned up. Quality press is emerging in many of the emerging markets now and the journalists who write for them are also young and bright with new ways of thinking and researching their materials.

CNN, MSNBC, BBC and their broadcast counterparts in the emerging market regions ensure that news is no longer kept out of most of the emerging markets. The global nature of the broadcast media is another factor that has brought considerable changes to the emerging markets. These more mature media also provide role modeling for the development of in country broadcast programming.

Web based communications are now at the tip of our fingers in many societies, including the emerging markets. We have witnessed for ourselves the impact of global news coverage in countries that were once isolated. Today, it is unrealistic to expect news to be kept beyond the reach of anyone with a desire or a need to know.

The challenges of communication are associated more with the culture of communication than with the availability of the means to communicate.

In the developed markets, there are conventions that drive the behavior associated with communication. Press releases are used by journalists as sources of information or news. They are not paid advertorials. In some emerging markets today, perhaps where it is still difficult to get hold of a newspaper or magazine, there can be an expectation that the publication of the content of the release must be paid for.

Typically, Western companies operating in emerging markets attempt to resist this paid advertising approach to featuring news stories about companies and business developments.

As existing publications evolve, new media emerge online and online services become readily available. The current generation of journalists is much more familiar with new technologies, has a greater knowledge and understanding of global markets and trends, and is rapidly becoming more able to communicate in English, now recognized as the world language for media. This also makes it much easier to bring media face to face with company leaders at home and abroad.

Equally, journalists in developing markets have greater access to new tools and resources that allow them to optimize communications. Face to face communication needs to be balanced with these tools, which can provide a great deal of information that needs sifting or interpretation. There is still no complete substitute for relationship building and regular contact with the press.

Journalists in some emerging markets expect to be paid to attend a news conference, and many company public/media relations professionals think nothing of providing travel money and other blandishments to encourage them to attend an event and cover it for their publications.

At a press conference in certain countries today, the journalists will happily ask the questions provided by the PR executives who invited them. And when they do write their articles, they will use the materials provided by the PR agency or in company executive, verbatim. Investigative and aggressive reporting are not yet developed in developing markets.

Relationship building is very much a factor in building an effective media network in the emerging markets. There is still a fine line to be drawn between the relationship building that is local custom and practice, and what might be characterized as corrupt practice. Gift giving to the media in an emerging market must be carefully managed. Media tours must likewise be handled ethically, so that there is a benefit to the company inviting the journalists to visit their global headquarters, as well as to the journalists making, what for them could be, a first trip out of their home country.

Misrepresentation in the media needs to be handled sensitively in some emerging markets. Local media can see an opportunity to extort from foreign companies considered to be rich, in order to sell more copies and ingratiate themselves with their local readership.

Translations and language adaptations have always been and remain challenging. Today, there are more and better translation services available, but it is incumbent on the PR executives responsible for releasing information to the media to be vigilant and monitor carefully the adapted content of any release or other means of external communication.

Public relations consultancies have been growing rapidly in number and size in many of the developing markets and provide a range of benefits both to the media and to the companies that seek media coverage. Large networked consultancies open subsidiaries and establish partnerships with local agencies. At the same time boutique agencies set up by entrepreneurs open their doors. They all contribute to raising the level of public and media relations, by bringing discipline and process to the interface between the press and the companies and organizations seeking to have their stories published. Agencies also identify the serious media and can make it much more cost effective to conduct PR in a developing country where the infrastructure may not yet be fully in place. They also provide a useful filter for companies that are often small in size with considerable business opportunities to manage.

In summary, the nature of communication has been evolving and continues to move forward as the boundaries that separated the emerging from the developed countries continue to break down. Modern technology is a major factor in speeding up and making communications universal. Now it is up to practitioners to raise their standards of professionalism and ethics, to establish the principles and checks and balances that guide us in the more developed parts of the world. One thing is certain; these changes are taking place much faster in the emerging markets than it took to make them in our more mature markets of the world."

Our corporate functions provide professional advice and support throughout all phases of entering and operating in emerging markets. It is indispensable for our businesses to use these services to ensure local compliance and to avoid risks, pitfalls and delays. They are also instrumental in assisting local corporate functions to be built up.

Chapter 11 - A New Challenge for Human Resources

The Initial Scenario

When doing business in emerging markets, human resources were challenged with new responsibilities that far exceeded its classic role in the Western world. We faced a mix of traditional tasks requiring expertise in setting up a human resources organization and handling transcultural issues that required our skills as consultants and facilitators. We also faced a new responsibility for facility management and operational business support. In addition, functions such as security, expatriate management and employee care required much more attention due to the nature of the emerging markets. We also had to take into account some critical success factors - coping with the complexity and diversity of the region, keeping up with the speed and growth of business demands, facing extended cycle times and complicated logistics and managing stand-alone situations. And of course, we had to be prepared for surprises.

The problems we faced in many developing countries were rather discouraging.

- A human resources culture and structure did not exist. Under the former regimes, personnel were an administrative function ensuring political discipline.

- The legacies of the former system still dominated large parts of daily life.

- The labor market was distorted. Clerical skills were overrated and scientific positions underpaid. There was no recognizable search and hiring mechanism.

- Compensation and benefit structures only prevailed in the state industry. Benchmarking samples and surveys were rare and unstable.

- Labor legislation was subject to frequent change. Interpretation by authorities was often protective and arbitrary.

- Employability of elderly people was rather limited. Many could not mentally adapt to the changes at hand.

- Universities were stuck with curricula not compatible with market demand.

- No support structure existed. Banks were not ready for cashless salary payment, and payroll was run manually.

- Local administration was entangled in the old bureaucracy.

What does it look like more than a decade later? Local governments and authorities, multinational corporations, law and public accounting firms, Western consulting firms, aid and support programs, and an army of Western and local professionals have turned the situation almost completely around.

- Human resources are increasingly a recognized and well-established function.

- Nations returned to their historical, intrinsic value systems.

- The labor market has stabilized to a certain degree, and professional search and hiring procedures are increasingly in place.

- External and internal compensation and benefit surveys are not yet as common as in the Western world, but are becoming more popular.

- Labor legislation was firmed up following Western models.

- A young, highly skilled and motivated workforce has emerged.

- Universities have formed partnerships with leading Western counterparts and modernized their curricula.

- Complex support infrastructures exist, and most bureaucrats have learned to relate to individuals as customers.

Nothing is perfect, and there is still plenty of room for further improvements. But the tremendous progress is impressive. Those HR professionals who were lucky to actively participate in this major change unanimously confirm that this was a unique opportunity and the best time of their careers.

"Every human resources professional should seize the opportunity to work in emerging markets," says Marcia Carey-Ray (Director of Human Resources, EMEA). "No other environment better challenges the character of the individual and his or her competencies. The experience requires HR professionals to understand and internalize the myriad of values, beliefs and customs that are often quite different from their own, while, at the same time, discovering ways to add value in all aspects of HR work. Although the concepts of HR practice provide a foundation from which to work, HR professionals in emerging markets must demonstrate an ability to think and solve problems differently. Standard practice is often replaced with a more localized approach that proves more effective. Cultural, political and socioeconomic dynamics of the country may cause the HR organization to totally rethink its approaches."

"Interpersonal skills and behavioral style play important roles in the acceptance of HR professionals who are 'imported' into emerging markets countries," Marcia continues. "It is the professional who is able to exercise listening, learning and observing skills who seems to integrate most quickly. The HR professional must be open to change and difference while staying in touch with his or her own values.

In addition, the HR professional is often cast into an extended role. Because most offices in emerging countries are staffed at minimum levels, HR professionals have to develop additional skills. It is not uncommon for HR to handle facilities management, government relations, safety and security, and even office management. Although these responsibilities add to an already demanding workload, they do place the HR professional at the center of activity, thus affording HR the opportunity to significantly influence the infrastructure and culture of the company's presence in a country.

Those HR professionals who 'graduate' from the experience have developed the ability to operate in what are often ambiguous situations requiring great creativity and flexibility. They also understand and appreciate the richness of cultures and belief systems different from their own. They can step outside the boundaries of traditional HR work and grow at a pace that is often more rapid and intense than their counterparts. The HR professional who accepts the challenging work of emerging markets will return from the experience as a different and enlightened person who will add significant value to the corporation in general," Marcia concludes.

Ten Key HR Issues

Over time we identified the following key issues requiring our special attention:

- Organization
- Vision as a premier employer
- Money

- Security, safety and health

- Management of expatriates

- Employee welfare

- Education

- Equal Opportunities and Affirmative Action

- Change Management

- Cultural Diversity

Organization. At the time we began penetrating emerging markets, a regional HR function was not typical for Motorola's culture. This had typically been a line responsibility in businesses. As discussed earlier, a role model was introduced to provide a dedicated HR resource to a virgin region. The concept has a three-dimensional structure: the HR departments of the businesses, corporate HR for the region, and the local HR departments in the major countries.

To prevent overlaps and conflicts of interest, we designed a matrix that clearly defines responsibilities. This complex structure assumes close coordination achieved through regular meetings of all HR staff engaged in the emerging markets. As a general guideline:

- Corporate HR assumes operational responsibility for those countries with no local HR function. Whenever critical mass justifies establishing local HR, corporate HR will step back and provide support, while local HR assumes operational HR responsibility.

- The local HR departments take care of the business-specific activities (i.e., recruitment) but are backed up by corporate HR. Corporate HR, in turn, acts as custodian of the company's key beliefs and values, implements overriding HR policies and procedures, and provides ongoing interface between the various parties involved.

- The HR departments of our business units coordinate their activities with the corporate and local HR organizations. Once a business has achieved a certain size and maturity in the country they normally establish their own HR which also may serve the smaller business on a shared service basis.

As regions, countries and our own organization progress, different Human Resources structures for the emerging markets are being implemented.

Vision as Premier Employer. The second key issue is the realization of our "premier employer" vision. Those who join our company have chosen a long-term relationship based on equal employment opportunities, pay for performance, career development, and lifelong learning. The challenge is that this philosophy cannot be conveyed in an interview or during employee orientation. People have to experience and internalize it over time, which underscores the need for effective retention practices to avoid losing the best talent.

Money. The third key issue is money. "The missing rationale of supply and demand in the labor market is a critical element," says Frank Andreutti (Rewards Manager, CEE / MEA). "For instance, bilingual secretaries in the early stages earned more than engineers. Such imbalances will only be corrected over time when clerical skills become massively available. All this generates a lot of fluctuations.

Another factor is the attitude toward money, which can be explained by history and culture. Under the former systems, there was no exposure to money in a free labor market. For the first time, people are confronted with the trade value of their work. This especially applies to the younger managers and professionals whose salary expectations might therefore be less conservative and controlled. High inflation and currency movements that cause the value of items and salaries to change constantly further confuse the situation.

When foreign companies enter emerging markets, they tend to export their values and judgment both morally and financially. As a result, even if companies originally hire an inexpensive workforce, they will have no problem granting substantial pay increases because the pay levels are still much lower than in the mother company. But a red flag is raised when local pay level reaches that of a low-cost Western country. If the motivation of a company has been cheap labor, they may relocate to another emerging market with an even lower cost level. The effect of such practices is obvious. It boosts local remuneration to such an extent that corporations with a firm compensation philosophy run into difficulties."

Security, Safety and Health. This is the fourth key issue and is derived from the eternal law that crime and health risks increase alongside liberalization, open borders and wealth. Therefore, upgrading our security, safety and health policies, procedures and processes is a top company priority.

Reuven Lanir (Security Director EMEA) emphasizes certain precautionary measures in the following guidelines.

"The foundation of a new business or joint venture and other startup activities should be preceded by a due diligence investigation," Reuven says. "It is wise to invest up front in such an effort rather than end up with big surprises or even risks later on."

In some countries, the distinction between business, politics and crime is sometimes blurred. The main concerns are fraudulent activity, criminal connections, lack of confidentiality and poor financial track records. "Without full evidence of our potential partner's funding, corporate history, business associates and litigation record, we may risk dealing with businesses that are either in financial difficulties or else involved in illegal or unethical activities," Reuven says.

Employees relocating, doing business and traveling out of their home countries into high-risk areas are a major concern to the company. Criminals view them as potential targets. They are considered rich, unable to communicate well and unfamiliar with the surroundings and local customs. Reuven warns against traveling alone into remote areas.

"Security risks do not stop at the front of the office or home door," he says. Each local office and facility should develop and keep a current crisis management and contingency plan. They should also install adequate physical security devices. Home security is even more critical since criminals prefer to deal with individuals and their families rather than with a collective office staff. It is also important to keep security in mind when planning special events.

Here is an enumeration of customary security programs and devices used by local organizations and business travelers:

- Travel assistance program: Provides a comprehensive source for international travel information and services.

- Listings of regional security offices of embassies, which offer local assistance in emerging countries.

- Intranet Security Web: Lists security, health and safety information for several hundred 300 cities and countries.

- Crisis prevention and management plans, which offer guidance in training, simulation exercises and tailored plans.

- Bomb threat plan: Generic samples and guidance in the development of such plans for offices and facilities.

- Country evacuation and emerging plan: A detailed framework for quick and effective handling of emergencies and evacuation in case of major events, such as a military coup.

- Travel medical kit: Designed to be carried with the traveler at all times, it contains first-aid supplies and sterile instruments for local medical treatment.

- SOS access card: Ensures prompt and professional medical and travel assistance in emerging cases by a global network of contacts.

- Blood care program: Entitles employees to receive emergency supplies of fully screened and tested blood products and sterile equipment.

- Travel care card: A plastic card that includes personal information of the employee in the event of illness or accident.

- Business Travel Accident (BTA) Program: Provides travel accident insurance covering accident, death, dismemberment and disability while traveling on company business.

- Global Business Travel Medical Program: Covers medical expenses incurred due to serious illness or injury during international business traveling.

We have purposely listed these programs and devices in detail because they are very important for the company and the traveler and may save lives. However, it must be mentioned that this listing is not complete. Information about additional programs may be obtained from ministries, airlines, travel agencies, banks and other sources.

Companies in the meantime have made tremendous progress in the fields of security, safety and health, according to Jim Baxter (Reuvin Lanir's predecessor). "I admired those Motorola employees and contractors working in areas in which only a few Westerns had worked before and under conditions which many did not fully understand," he says. He quickly found that those working in the more dangerous environments desperately wanted information on security and safety issues that they had never faced and for which they had not been prepared. "The lack of preparation was simply because no one had asked any serious questions and the governing local authorities had not made us, or any other Western company, aware of the real day-to-day working conditions," Jim says. "A number of such dangerous assignments could have been avoided if management and the employees had been more aware of the potential risks."

It is a sad fact of life that bad news dominates the media because good news is not deemed exciting and interesting enough. As far as security is concerned, only an insignificant part of the population is involved in crime and violence, but this minority makes up the vast majority of the news. This kind of coverage is unjustifiably clouding the bright skies over our emerging markets.

Management of Our Expatriates. Corporations frequently underestimate the importance and problematic nature of expatriate assignments. There are even reports of occasional disregard and mistreatment of employees who are willing to give up their safe, comfortable home environments to help bail a company out of trouble in a foreign and sometimes hostile location. Not only that, but if these employees repatriate, they may end up waiting for a position because they were simply forgotten. Even worse, they might find their social security and pension entitlements have been forfeited.

Special attention is therefore paid to a professional expatriate management to ensure global mobility. It addresses the following issues:

- Provide guidance and support to business management and human resources in the selection, expatriation and repatriation of managers and professionals for and on special assignments.

- Deliver information, consultation and coordinated services to expatriates and their families prior to, during and after the assignments. This pertains to: cross-cultural orientation; immigration and relocation; document requirements; accommodation and housing; local hiring conditions; local services, such as medical, banking and shopping; schooling and educational services; language requirements; tax, social security, insurance and pensions; career development and lifestyle issues; occupational opportunities for spouses; and the repatriation process.

- Ensure ongoing interface between organizations and individuals involved in expatriate management, such as business managers, human resources, local offices, public accountants, law firms, fiscal offices and immigration authorities.

- Act as custodian of Motorola's expatriate policies and assist in adjusting its terms and conditions to host country changes.

Victor Polarny (Business Development Manager Russi) was asked to relocate from Moscow to Novosibirsk, an interesting variation of our customary relocation process. I spent a full day with him in our Moscow office, and we jointly developed a detailed action plan covering office search, lease and facilitation, local staffing and his own expatriation. He took ownership of the plan and managed it by himself with our remote help. "Once you have a good plan and have confidence in it, things become relatively easy," Victor confirms.

Employee Welfare. Another key issue is employee welfare. Many local people were not capable of dealing adequately with the stress of change and became panic stricken. Western people, in turn, were exposed to stressful stand-alone situations, robbery, blackmail attempts and other forms of crime.

This is the ugly side of emerging markets. Such real-life incidents challenge human resilience. In response, Motorola's Employee Assistance Programs were recently expanded to cover the emerging markets. Their purpose is to develop the infrastructure needed to perform confidential, behavioral and mental health consulting and counseling.

Education: Asset or Shortfall? In the initial start-up of an emerging market human resources is usually faced with a mismatch between the educational profile of the country and the business requirements. The main reasons are the impositions of the political system, hierarchical structures, low per capita incomes and an underestimation of the vital role of education for social development and economic growth.

In communist and socialist countries education was always subordinate to political goals and riddled with ideology. This resulted in an abundance of technical talent but a critical shortage of business skills.

We visited the University of Zelenograd, the Silicon Valley of Russia near Moscow. They practiced a closed loop system, whereby students rotated in semester intervals between the university and a nearby semi-contractor plant. They were offered an up-front job guarantee after their final examinations. The housing they were offered as part of the deal was far above Russian standards. In this way, the party bred a dedicated technical elite.

In South Africa the black population had been excluded from white schools. The consequences of this could be clearly seen in the dramatic shortage of professional and managerial qualifications. In Central Africa education had received a low priority in the post-colonial period, and the missing industrial base caused a lack of technical skills. As the old colonial networks are still alive so are many of the managerial and professional positions held by the former military and mercenary force.

The traditional cultures and hierarchical structures represented a hurdle for a universal education system in the Middle East and Asia. Especially in the Middle East the labor market is dominated by immigrants and expatriates, whilst the upper level positions are reserved for an elite educated at Western universities. In both regions the craftsmanship skills passed down from generation to generation had formed the backbone of society over many centuries.

In the Latin America of the old days, eligibility for higher level education was largely dependent on the political conformity and the financial status of the family.

In the meantime most states have recognized the vital role of education for their future survival and are heavily investing in this field as proven by the high number of excellent graduates in modern disciplines such as information technology. Especially in Asia, substantial progress in building a sophisticated educational system can be observed. A keen spirit to adapt and learn shown in these countries supports these changes.

Equal Employment Opportunities and Affirmative Action. The eighth HR issue is to provide equal opportunities and affirmative action. Motorola is an equal employment opportunities/affirmative action employer. To this end we are globally committed to eliminate the vast inequalities and discrimination regarding race, gender and minority groups. Large parts of the world are still suffering from this burden, which affects societies, families and individuals. Corporations, in turn, are handicapped by a shortage of human resources. Apartheid in South Africa, for instance, marginalized entire population groups with black women being the worst affected. People in emerging markets are particularly disadvantaged, since low levels of income, status and perspective further aggravate the existing low general standard.

Not long ago the human resources organization of China launched a gender diversity project unique in Asian culture and tradition and ambitious in terms of numbers. Its objective was to raise the number of female exempt employees to 40 per cent within five years. Motorola recognized that a diverse workforce would provide a cutting edge in the light of the limited human resources. Benchmarking results revealed that only a few multinational corporations are pursuing gender diversity in Asia. The benefits are obvious: Internally this will increase productivity, motivation and retention. Our external partners will deal with a more skilled and sophisticated workforce. Most importantly, this program will support our key beliefs and values.

Building on a gender diversity base line the HR team developed a relevant strategy and a range of tools to steer the process. Assessment centers were created to identify new and experienced candidates for a female candidate pool, training and development programs were set up, compensation models were designed and internal and external communications packages were developed. Progress was controlled by deliverable deadlines.

The gender diversity program also provided other benefits. The processes developed were also applied to human asset planning while team members improved their participative management skills. We also received wide public attention.

Yan Keng Chong (HR Director Semiconductors, AP) comments on this major initiative: "China represents one of the most potential growth countries for Motorola in Asia. Leadership supply and localization is a critical process to ensure that we have the right talent in the right place. This gender diversity initiative enables us to have access to all sources of leadership capability within China. We hope that with the lessons learnt from this initiative started in China that success strategies can subsequently be applied to similar initiatives throughout the rest of Asia."

Change Management. At the beginning of this chapter, we experienced a brief insight into the complexity of change. Regions and countries subject to transition require our HR people to act as change agents. This section deals with the transition process of an entire region and the way HR coped with it.

Motorola's presence in Latin America goes back more than 45 years. Our presence in the past, however, was limited due to the regions historically less stable economic and political conditions, and several unsuccessful attempts to grow in the region, creating an atmosphere of caution. Now there are new times for both Latin America and foreign investors in as far as the region represents one of the greatest growth opportunities in the field of telecommunications and electronics. Governments, eager to gain access to modern technology, are opening their markets to encourage foreign investors and have made the region the avant-garde of regulatory change.

Each country, however, was in a different stage of development and transition. Listed below are some of the conditions affecting Human Resources:

- Management style and practice greatly varied depending on cultural and social environment.

- Unions were observed to move into a less restricted climate with a somewhat disorganized agenda.

- Governments appeared to retain a paternalistic attitude towards employee rights with the trend towards a mandated works environment.

- Government intervention with compensation and benefits continued to add substantial overhead costs and prevented performance related policies.

- The inflation psychology permeated every aspect of the employees' life - people therefore took a rather short-term perspective of pay to protect their purchasing power.

The Human Resources team under the leadership of Dan Nickel (Senior Vice President, Human Resources, LAC, for a large business unit) recognized that dealing with all these complex issues would require a concerted effort and structured approach. They selected a tool, which is used by Motorola businesses to plan their future on a revolving basis: the Long-Range Plan (LRP). The approach was as eager as unique in view of the heterogeneity of the regions and the wealth of burning issues.

Guided by a mission statement the team identified the following key issues to be adhered to as a priority:

- Improve productivity to enable Motorola to be competitive in all its core competencies.

- Upgrade the quality of people and form a nucleus of future regional and local leaders.

- Provide organizations that are efficient and allow sharing of resources, know how and learning.

- Develop compensation and benefit structures, which are competitive, performance driven and are restoring the value of money in an inflationary environment.

- Form a management style that is built on our values and empowerment and participation of people.

- Design labor relations policies, which anticipate the new role of the external labor parties and with the goal of maintaining Motorola's labor relations position.

Dan Nickel summarizes "I was responsible for Human Resources in Latin America from 1990 through 1998, a period of rapid change. We were not only faced with a multitude of action items, but also an environment with diverse cultures, varying degrees of economic development, many political ups and downs, social unrest and last but not least the need to realign our own organization".

It was only because of these stringent programs and a concerted team effort that this complex project could be realized over time.

Cultural Diversity. The final HR issue presented in this book (in reality there are many more) is cultural diversity. There are 191 countries on our globe, which means hundreds of different cultures. These cultures are not linked by borders, since they are artificially drawn while cultures have naturally grown. In our operations we employ a workforce that reflects this cultural diversity with all its behavior patterns. People don't deposit their culture at the factory or office door but internalize it in their work and relationships.

For us as human resources and business people it is not only a question of courtesy and respect to engage ourselves with these cultures but also a matter of our acceptance and success in the local environment.

Motorola's relevant policies promote the spirit of human dignity and constant respect for people. As custodians of these policies, it is also our responsibility to lead our businesses through these processes.

Ratana Zahn (Executive Secretary in our German company) describes some of the cultural facets of her home country, Thailand, but they also represent other Asian countries.

"Thailand means 'land of the free', and throughout its 800 year history Thailand can boast the distinction of being the only country in south-east Asia never to have been colonized.

Increased and extended education is needed to support Thailand in the transformation from an agricultural to an industrial country. Traditional rural life is becoming more urban. The Thai people thus need different skills than 20 years ago to adapt to these changes. To ensure this takes place, much power must be decentralized into local communities so that curricula can be adapted to the needs of the people.

Children are always taught to honor their parents and be grateful to them for the time and money spent on education. This fact demonstrates the hierarchical nature of Thai family life.

Traditionally, children lived not far from their parents and gave them a substantial part of their income. After a working career there is no pension is Thailand. Thus, the support of children is necessary for survival. The Western idea of placing old people in nursing homes is an alien concept. They consider it an affront to their parents who have invested their lives in their children.

With industrialization however, many young Thai people have moved away from home to urban areas, and although they still support their parents the influence of their elders is waning. Traditionally parents would have chosen a partner for their children, now young people tend to choose for themselves.

Thai life is influenced strongly by the Buddhist religion. It is a polite culture based on non-confrontation. Public dispute, criticism or signs of impatience or anger are interpreted as lack of self-control or weakness.

Rapid progress of society causes an increasing difference in lifestyle and expectation levels between the elder and younger generations. This is reflected in our workforces as well. The subject therefore deserves much more attention than in a typical western company. It requires our HR professionals to sensitively deal with tradition and progress under one roof."

The Bird in a Cage. It is a fact of life that people, who are hindered in using their skills by a political or economic system, develop a remarkable capability to work around it. They create booming black economies, which help them survive. Bypassing the system almost becomes a type of sport.

We once had a business dinner in a local currency restaurant in Moscow. Such restaurants and also shops were based on a government policy to back up local currency. After having paid the bill in rubles our interpreter urged me to go to the backyard where I would meet a very important person. It was the waiter who returned my rubles and collected the equivalent in dollars. After dinner I ordered a taxi to the hotel. Out of nowhere a small army bus appeared and picked me up. On the way other passengers joined me. I learned that this was a shuttle bus service organized by the soldiers to make a quick dollar.

People had adapted quickly but in the wrong direction. In the initial euphoria of change many people wanted to break out of the mold but ended up behaving like a bird in a cage which had forgotten how to fly when finally the cage door opened.

Having worked all your life in such an environment it is difficult to become a market economy manager overnight, dealing with total customer satisfaction, quality improvement, cycle time reduction, organizational efficiency, marketing strategy and corporate culture. A shortage of critical skills such as general business management, marketing, sales, finance, human resources, quality and others characterized this scenario.

Often people were stuck in the middle of the transformation process. The old system had not yet completely disappeared and the new system had not yet gained a foothold. This required patience and empathy on the part of their Western counterparts. If, for any reason, we would have been the ones forced to switch from a market to a command economy how long would it have taken us to adapt?

The people were not only highly interested in the market economy, but they carried high expectations of this system in them. At special request I delivered a speech to the Czech Society for Quality Management. The participants, all high level managers, were rather astonished to hear that it took Motorola almost ten years to implement our six-sigma program throughout our organizations. I explained to them that the ideas had to first grow in people's hearts. Some of the managers had tried to impose a quality program in their companies within a few months but were dismayed at the lack of response. This is just one example displaying the positive impatience in all regions.

Walk as You Talk. To support the people in their difficult transition process, it is important to prove to them that we mean it seriously. Karl Heinz Paulitschke (Director of Human Resources, CEE / MEA) addresses a specific type of behavior crucial to our success not only in relation to human resources but also to all businessmen.

"Emerging countries provide managers and employees with challenges nobody can ever experience in established countries.

In order to fulfill your task, you have to be student and teacher at the same time. You have to learn from the new country and its people whenever possible. You have to be humble, throw all arrogance overboard and understand the demands and needs of the people and country and take the cultural differences into consideration.

That does not mean that you compromise the company's culture, ethics and values, but you have to recognize where the new partners come from, what their historical experience and background is and you have to overcome a natural mistrust and handle naivity.

The backlog of life in a lot of countries is immense and has to be understood. A lot has to change within a few years, when others have needed half a century.

While teaching and discussing our human resources and business systems, everybody is viewed as a role model by the new employees and managers. The bad experiences they have lived through or are still going through with governments or other bodies cause them to draw comparisons. It is very important that we walk as we talk and really live up to what we say and expect from others.

Our example influences the behavior of our partners. We are the window between these two worlds."

In emerging markets the Human Resources function plays a double role as advocate of the people and change agent in the process. This places a high demand on the professionals but enables them to add significant value to their own curriculum and to the corporation.

Chapter 12 - Looking Backward and Looking Forward

Once a company has completed a number of business launches, it is time to review what they did right and what went wrong. This will allow them to determine the future direction.

What Have We Done Right and Wrong?

Dedicated Resource. As previously described, we created an empowered emerging market staff and teams, which operated throughout all phases of market entry in a total systems approach. This strategy enabled us to concentrate on the real issues without becoming entangled in the traditional organizational structure and to demonstrate a strong commitment to our local partners.

Business Migration. Secondly, we followed the logic of the business migration pattern typical for new markets. This prevented us from taking the second step before the first one, allowed us to move along a structured path, and maintained our direction and progress with proper speed. It also created high synergy and enhanced our corporate identity. Furthermore, sharing our learning, know-how and resources became a recipe for our rapid progress.

If we observe business migration over a longer period of time and with a larger sample of corporations, a pattern becomes evident. This is not the only model because the original strategic intent or changing business priorities may dictate another sequence and timing of events. Nevertheless, I offer this model as a rough guideline, which served us well as we built our presence in emerging markets (See Figure 16, Business Migration).

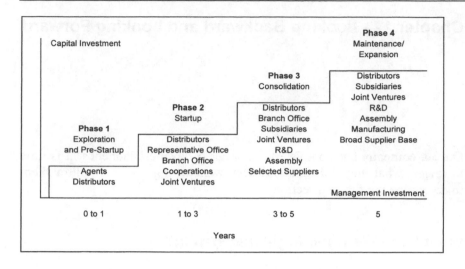

Figure 16: Business Migration

Added Value Strategy. Added value programs are a catalyst for an accelerated market entry. They are door openers to key publics and offer a range of initial benefits. Moreover, they demonstrate commitment and seriousness towards our partners.

Turning Barriers into Opportunities. We experienced that barriers are seldom twists of fate to be accepted but are worth being challenged. Conversely, we recognized that opportunities tended to fall back into the status of barriers if not properly managed. We therefore reviewed each barrier and opportunity in the light of the following questions:

- Are there opportunities, which may turn into barriers?

- Are there barriers that may turn into opportunities?

- Which measures can be taken to convert a barrier into an opportunity?

- Are opportunities or barriers applicable to the company as a whole or only to certain businesses?

- Is it worthwhile accepting a barrier and working around it instead of doing nothing?

- How can opportunities be strengthened further and barriers be overcome?

When a leading fast food company started up in Russia, many of the local products did not meet their worldwide specifications. They bought a local farm, bred their own cattle and cultivated their own food products. They, thus, turned a barrier into an opportunity, generating local employment and developing a successful business with many happy customers.

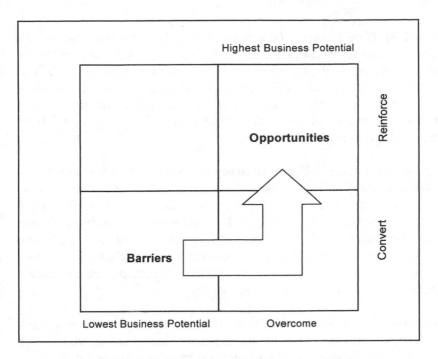

Figure 17: Turning Barriers Into Opportunities

On the front line of business, one of the frequent barriers was an exaggerated expectation level on the part of the local partners. Dealing with multinational corporations was often perceived as catching a big fish or milking a cash cow. One of the standard opening questions in negotiations was: When do you start manufacturing locally and how many people will you employ? It required a high degree of diplomatic skills to help our counterparts understand that sales are only one element in the added value chain of a long customer/supplier relationship. And local employment does not only mean a job, but also the benefit of sharing a premier employer concept for best-in-class people. Once we could convince people that local content may be delivered by investments other than local manufacturing, this barrier could usually be turned around into an opportunity.

We became witnesses of this philosophy. At a Chinese/Western business dinner there was a beautifully decorated table for two people in the middle of the room. The chairs stood empty. The Chinese dinner speaker explained the reason: The symbolic arrangement was dedicated to the two most important people in any company: the customer and the supplier. This insight was more meaningful than a one-week training course on this subject.

Mapping of Time Frames. Throughout the early years, we more or less applied a sequential process, meaning that each step was taken after the other. That meant we neglected to consider such time delays as the office registration, hiring initial staff, type approvals and bureaucratic hurdles. However, this was corrected by critical path mapping, saving between three and six months of cycle time (See Figure 18, Mapping of Time Frames: Critical Path Method).

The Appropriate Legal Form. In many countries, we started with a representative office. This legal structure has some built-in limitations. For instance, it does not accommodate typical sales office activities such as signing sales contracts, issuing billings and invoices, and performing customer service. This situation also discouraged our newly hired sales staff who had to restrain their energy. For these reasons, we now select a legal structure that promotes rather than hinders business, especially since changing the registration may be expensive and lengthy.

Which Office Size? Some of our first offices were not planned for growth because of low business expectations, expensive leases and the risk of idle space. Suddenly, business increased, we outgrew the space and were faced with additional space needs. This resulted in some expensive and time-consuming relocation that could have been avoided by more aggressive planning. Now we factor in reasonable growth expectations.

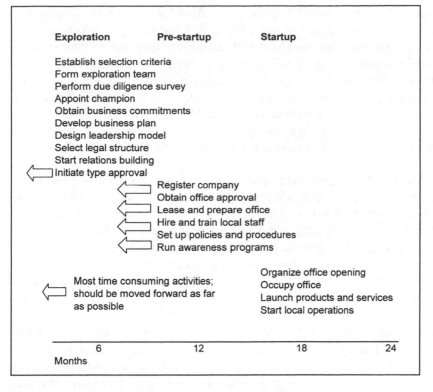

Figure 18: Mapping of Time Frames: Critical Path Method

Timing of Awareness Programs. Our first road show took place well before we established a local presence. Thus, the high awareness and expectation declined because there was no timely follow-up. In some cases, the initial positive acceptance turned negative because we had shown up with a flagship and then disappeared like a submarine. The lesson learned was that the office opening should closely follow any country event.

The Critical Stand-Alone Period. Occasionally, the local area network was not yet ready at the time of the office occupation. The reasons ranged from organizational problems to lack of local expertise and suppliers. The result was that the office was cut off from the rest of the corporation and practically non-operational. Through a concerted effort, this problem was solved and is no longer an issue of concern.

When to Invest in Local Support. We found out by painful experience that a local support function must be established before a critical mass is reached. The lead time involved in local hiring, training, accommodating the position and setting up policies and procedures is at least twice as long as in the Western world. Ideally, critical functions such as Finance and Human Resources should be part of the initial staff because the startup work is the same for 10 people as it is for 100. We have had success in assigning an experienced Western professional for a period of three to six months to the local office to support, coach and counsel the local hires.

Up-Front Policies and Procedures. Policies and procedures need to be carefully scrutinized and adjusted before they are put into effect in an emerging market operation. They must comply with local legislation, culture and practices. The office must translate the policies and train employees. Lack of policy is painful and costly. A good pro-active plan limits this damage. For example, a salary mistake for a new hire that could have been avoided with a salary structure may have to be carried through the system for some years before it is corrected.

What Is the Conclusion? What did we gain from these mistakes? First of all, they cannot be totally avoided whenever we enter unknown territory and start from zero. We had to experiment and try new things that others had not done before in order to progress in our emerging markets. We preferred to take a risk rather than just wait and see. This is the challenge for pioneers, and we voluntarily took it up, knowing that, by trial and error quite a few corporations had become very successful and many inventions had been created.

No Blueprint for the Future

Many Events Are Unpredictable. Once a company has worked through all four business phases (or even earlier) it is appropriate to adjust plans to new global, regional or country developments. This may require that we re-direct our business or even re-position the entire corporation. It is wise to initiate such changes as early as possible because, like a big steamship, the company will take some time and distance to alter course.

The Titanic crew oversaw the early warning signals for the icebergs. Russia lost its leading position after World War I because it internalized its resources instead of globalizing them. The European car industry, with the mountains on their doorstep, neglected the design of four wheel drive cars, which came firstly with importing from the Japanese. Such fundamental mistakes are irreversible.

An optimistic scenario may quickly change into a pessimistic one and ruin investment plans, as in the case of Iraq. The sharply rising oil demand in fast developing economies like China is boosting the prices at a level which is non affordable to many consumers in the emerging markets. The development of alternative energies, however, is being neglected.

Here are two such scenarios, in which even governments do not seem to have a blueprint for the future and are requested to review their policy. Carlos Baradello (General Manager Market and Business Platforms, LAC region) describes some of the political and demographic paradigm shiftings between the United States and Latin America. An interesting perspective for Europe's future is described following the Latin American report.

Latin America in the New Millennium. As we started the new millennium it became clear that most of the advances of the 1990's were now regressing. The attack on the World Trade Center on September 11, 2001, derailed the summit between Presidents George W. Bush and Vicente Fox of Mexico, which intended to bring new energy to the Western Hemisphere and the North/South Agenda. Since then, the economic recession and the increased focus on other urgent areas of the world (Afghanistan, Iraq, North Korea etc.) has caused the US agenda to make only limited progress in the field of the economic development and integration into the Western Hemisphere.

However, as the current urgent problems regain "normality" the Washington policy pendulum will return to the focus of the Western Hemisphere. In the meantime, however, the US will have to face a major transformation in its own domestic demographics. The Hispanic population in the US has become the largest ethnic minority, with an official population of 35.3 million (12.5% of the total US population). In fact, the actual number is closer to 45 million when undocumented Hispanic residents are included. Furthermore, the Hispanic ethnic group is to become the absolute majority in major states such as California and Texas over the next 15-20 years.

This new phenomenon will add a renewed emphasis to the North/South relations in the Western Hemisphere and provide new opportunities for economic development and market growth. In addition to the growing political influence of the Hispanic minority residents in the US as a group, its economic weight is reaching critical impact. For example, during 2002 the remittances of money into Latin America by Hispanics living in the US reached $33 billion to almost match the Foreign Direct Investment ($35 billion) going into the region during the same year.

The extension of the Free Trade Agreements with Mexico and the one in progress with Chile brings additional hope to the entire region's economic growth and a projected market integration of one billion consumers by 2006. Hopefully, we will not need to wait for another decade, rather as time compresses in the wireless internet age, the next few years can become the beginning of decades of LAC Region growth and Motorola can pick up the double digit growth left off in 2000. This renewed confidence in the form of promises of new growth opportunities in the Latin America and Caribbean region will help Motorola and other corporations' strategies materialize their hopes and aspirations.

From Old to New Europe. The recent integration of most Central- and Eastern European states into the European Union will abolish the memory of former borders. Millions of people will enjoy the free flow of capital, goods and labor and free choice of place of residence. This will cause a migration wave from East to West and of goods and capital from West to East. It will also be a potential source of possible labor conflicts, as increased immigration will mean a yet further overburdening of systems of social security in the West.

The rigid impositions of the European Union will force the Eastern countries to implement stringent political and economic reforms. In the end, a huge consumer market of over 450 million people will generate much incremental business.

The EU membership applied for by Turkey will strengthen Europe's geo-strategic position. With a 70% Islamic population share, it will enhance cultural integration between the Orient and Occident but will also provide the breeding ground for potential ethnic conflicts. In the southern parts of Europe, such as on the Italian, French and Spanish Mediterranean coasts, we notice an increasing immigration wave from Africa.

As a matter of fact, Europe is re-importing some of the emerging market problems into its own countries.

Growing the Growing Corporation

"Since our entrance in emerging market countries, Motorola has recognized their huge growth potential," says Gerry Lukomski (Director, CEE / MEA). "We had to patiently invest in those regions and be willing to stay in them for the long run, and in some countries we have been more successful than in others. But as a whole, these emerging markets are now adding significantly to our growth."

The size is projected to be in billions of dollars over the next decades and will require a concerted effort to ensure we gain a large share. "Motorola is actively and enthusiastically pursuing the opportunities in these developing countries presently and for the future," Gerry says. "We plan to continue to be a major player in these regions for many years to come."

None of what you have read in the previous chapters is possible without the right people. While having the right people at the corporate level is important, hiring the best local people is key. Patrick Canavan (Senior Vice President Global Governance) identifies four critical skills for local hires.

- The ability to properly balance interests between the customer and the company, to help the customer through our organizations and the company through the country bureaucracy.

- Technical competence to be able to convey to the customer the spectrum of our technical capabilities and to understand his or her technical needs.

- English language proficiency.

- Effective dealing at various country and customer levels to achieve local customer satisfaction but, at the same time, negotiate those terms and conditions that we need or desire.

Pat also points out several factors critical to the company's success in emerging markets.

- The capability of attracting the best university graduates through a sustained university relations program in the form of sponsoring faculty research, providing stipends and scholarships, and donating technical equipment to enhance brand awareness.

- An efficient human-resources planning process that is simple and flexible enough that business people are willing to go through the exercise but that provides the quality of data needed for targeted hiring and training.

- A skills-development framework to identify and teach those skills critical to organizational efficiency but not available in the country due to the different educational direction in the past.

- A retention program to stay ahead of the highly competitive labor market based on an innovative, premier employer concept such as creative compensation and benefit packages, and a career planning and development program.

- A sustained memorandum of understanding (MOU) process to identify the key strategic country issues and convert them into action plans with the intent to bring the company forward in the country on the whole.

With these processes in place, a company is ready to unlock new potentials in emerging markets. Yet many companies have not yet fully realized the hidden potential of emerging markets and still need to embrace this new reality. "At the higher levels, the emerging markets are perceived just as that: local, very profitable markets," Pat says. "In essence, they see them only on the surface -millions of people, so much GDP, so much pushed-up demand for Western products, systems and services. And they do not see them as resources for their own world-class development. They are not perceived as sources of new ideas or great and unimaginable talent for evolution and rapid growth. Nor do they view them as the nucleus of the next generation of engineering, marketing or business leaders.

"Management needs to let go of the image of emerging market employees as 'in service' to our existing portfolio and begin viewing them as part of a single generation. They are the leadership of the corporation in the year 2010. And if they are not leading our corporation, they'll be leading somebody else's corporation or their own."

Over time, some of Motorola's technological breakthroughs will come from these regions and people, who will enrich us with their talent and ideas.

A Regional Update

Looking back and looking forward also means to periodically review our return on commitment and investment. It is now fifteen years ago that the political, economic and social changes started in Central and Eastern Europe, South Africa and parts of the Middle East. Heinrich Korte (Human Resources Director Germany, CEE / MEA), summarizes what happened and did not happen during this time span.

"Nowadays, corporations should be glad to have the emerging markets as a growth engine. Outsourcing and off-shoring is taking place as slow growth in developed countries is overcome by cost-cutting. Growth strategy now means emerging markets strategy for many companies.

Many regions in Africa are still focusing on internal issues, and are not utilizing the potential market power of their huge population. If their leadership issues and social crises could be defeated, there would be enormous potential, due to the low economic level the majority would be starting from.

The Middle East is viewed by many people as being a dangerous area to work in. Our hotel office in Bagdad, for example, was completely destroyed by a bomb. Fortunately, we had relocated our employees some time before. Peace between Israel and Palestine would be the start of a booming area with a lot of wealth and intelligence. Peace will come for sure, but nobody knows when, so multinationals are still cautious with serious investments.

This is not the case with Central and Eastern Europe. Russia offers a huge market and resource capability and there are many other smaller Central and Eastern European countries which have become EU members or will do so in the future. Russia is on the right track, accepting a free economy is definitely their future. However, they still have a long bumpy road before them and politicians sometimes do not really understand that investments require stable and reliable political decisions. Yet the size of the market and the low cost of human resources still make the MNC's hot to invest. A population with increasing spending capability, demanding the latest technology and walking two steps at once in many areas is an advantage. But the second advantage may be even more important, namely the availability of resources! There are a huge number of highly-educated young people, eager to develop their homeland. For companies investing over there, this means that the cost of a labor force with a university degree, some years of experience and workable English language skills is less than in India. Moreover, locals are not looking for a green-card. They are proud of their country, want to stay and are motivated to develop their country into a bright future. While Moscow is the city-to-be for market access, the real advantage for the utilization of human resources lies outside the capital. St. Petersburg is much cheaper, the universities deliver outstanding talent and the infrastructure is good. Many companies have already recognized this so labor rates are increasing. Other cities south of Moscow will be the next hot-spots. However it is important that the country prevents any further deterioration of education, particularly as teachers are state-employees and are therefore at the lower end of the pay scale. The high oil price is, at least for Russia, currently a positive source of wealth and will be so for the next years.

Some other countries in the region are on the same track. Looking at the Ukraine, Kiev University is one of the biggest technical universities in Europe and infrastructure is getting better every day. There are more countries which are worth mentioning, but I will only give some examples here: Romania, with its great labor capability and well-educated technical background, or Turkey with both a huge market and a good labor force. Countries, some years ago counted under CEE, have developed even further: Hungary, the Czech Republic or Poland, at least in their main cities, look like Western countries. The appetite for consumption has made them valuable markets, while labor rates still remain far below average.

So, what is different today compared to the starting years of doing business in CEE? The development certainly took longer than originally anticipated, and it wasn't always clear which step to take next. Technical issues need money to get solved but are relatively easy to overcome. The mentality of the people is very positive towards the change and development of their homeland, but old thinking, old political ideas and even corruption create some challenges. Every day we move forward, markets grow and politicians and voters can see that the economic development is delivering higher standards of living. We can still expect critical observers as people are proud and don't take everything coming from the West as automatically being the best. Work with them as respected partners and you will earn trust and long-lasting relationships!"

Which conclusions can we draw from this scenario? As already stated, the process took much longer than envisaged. Change has to be internalized in the minds of people, a process much more complex than resolving technical issues.

While the generation involved in the transition deserves our full respect for their contributions, it will be the present young generation and their successors who will close a memorable chapter of recent history.

As far as markets are concerned, governments and corporations need to redirect their activities. Regions and countries move ahead at different speed and intensity. Some don't move on at all or even fall back. The latter two categories will deserve our attention and care in the future. While the big cities have been our first natural target, emphasis will shift to the rural area with a lot of hidden potential but also large territories.

Even after many years of engagement in the emerging markets, we are still in the middle of our learning curve. At this stage it makes sense to review our performance and draw the proper conclusions for our future work. While we had to frequently adjust our priorities to the varying degrees of transformation, the human resources potential turned out to be the backbone of our progress.

Chapter 13 - Different Regions - One Mission

A Comprehensive Approach

In the previous chapter we have analyzed our bottom line performance. In this context it is appropriate to also review how a company positions itself at a global level. Emerging markets conditions in the world regions vary greatly due to internal and external factors. For a company it is occasionally difficult to find a flexible response to these conditions but also to not sacrifice corporate identity and appear as a confederation of independent companies. If we compare the strategies and processes applied to market entry, however, a high similarity becomes apparent. In fact, there are more common than different patterns. This particularly applies to:

- A mission

- A total systems approach

- A structured market entry

- Special funding

- Sharing know-how and resources

- The added value strategies

- The awareness programs

- Training and education

We have identified three reasons for this cohesion: The globalization of internal and external networks enables an instant exchange of ideas. Many of the models have been designed for global use from the outset. Finally, quite a few are not new or magic. They have just been re-invented for a specific scenario or simply represent common business sense. It is not the amount of raw material which distinguishes a good car but the ingenious way in which it is assembled. The highest common denominator is found to be a company's mission for the emerging markets. The typical framework for such a mission is summarized as follows: "Our company is dedicated to actively participating in the development of the emerging markets to create prosperity for the countries and their population. To achieve this, we will invest our know-how and resources to a maximum extent and will share these with our local partners. In return we will gain access to new opportunities, allowing us to grow our own business to the benefit of our domestic and global obligations." The following business cases are examples of a comprehensive and synergetic regional strategy in compliance with the mission.

El Dorado, a Key Initiative in Latin America. Carlos Baradello describes a market strategy that opens new opportunities and offers tangible benefits to both the company and the region. It also highlights how to activate with a concerted effort the enormous human resources potential in an entire region.

"With the advent of the 1990's, Latin America recovered from the lost decade of the 1980's which had been punished with hyperinflation, economic stagnation, social unrest and limited economic growth.

The new winds of the 1990's brought democratically elected governments and the rules of market economy to most Latin American countries. The neo-liberal economic policies of Chile permeated east across the Andes into Argentina, north to Peru and Ecuador and across the Iguazú Falls into Brazil and many other countries. More specifically, the liberalization of telecom regulations and the privatization of the government owned public services (i.e. telephone, electricity, airports, and many other companies) brought enormous opportunities for growth to the telecommunications sector and related markets served by Motorola.

By summer in Buenos Aires in November of 1997 as the dot.com revolution was gaining momentum in Silicon Valley, Motorola's Board of Directors was preparing to meet in Argentina. This historic meeting, the first in Motorola history, not only brought visibility to Latin America and Caribbean (LAC) Region within the corporation, but during the meeting a key initiative of corporate renewal with exclusive focus in this region was approved: El Dorado.

Motorola anticipated the accelerated demand for communications products and services, which incorporated advanced technologies and increased the ability of businesses and individuals to communicate, manage their affairs and therefore be more productive. This hypothesis turned out to be right, and telecommunications was indeed one of the key engines for accelerated growth for most of the decade. However, it became apparent that the technology adoption would not follow the same model as in North America or Europe. Some phases would be skipped; others would be introduced earlier while others later or never at all."

The LAC Region gained importance as the telecommunications market exploded. The El Dorado founding fathers, who were rooted in the 10 x 2 ($10 billion revenues by 2002) initiative, concluded that unique rewards would be granted to specific corporations. These corporations would be able to play in the LAC indigenous local markets as a 'local company' offering products and services targeted to its unique needs and characteristics. This additional strength as an incumbent would create additional barriers of entry to potential new entrants, particularly new foreign competitors intending to penetrate this newly discovered market.

El Dorado was meant to seek strategic differentiation with the creation of 'native' affordable products, which met the regional customs, wants, desires and aspirations.

This increased market traction will in turn benefit the corporation in several ways:

- Accelerated growth of revenues due to products and services with a unique market advantage.

- Increased recognition of Motorola as 'local brand'.

- Improved market share and market intelligence.

- Creation of 'Regional Intellectual Property'.

The demographics of this market were of particular interest because of two specific reasons: 1) other regions of the world were aging rapidly (about 60% of the market was under 25) and 2) the heavy population density in urban areas. For example, four metropolitan areas in the El Dorado corridor (Santiago, Buenos Aires, Rio and Sao Paulo) are the home to over 75 million inhabitants.

El Dorado became a visible milestone of the work of many before and after its inception. I had the privilege to lead the organization from its institutional form (starting February 1989) when I was recruited by the Regional President and Regional Human Resources Director. The following three years were an exceptional time in my professional career, when significant contributions and lessons were acquired by a small team of highly committed and dedicated individuals, and the unwavering support of my direct supervisor Carlos Genardini, LAC Region President.

Of the many activities and the multiple businesses we tackled, there was one, which enhanced Motorola's presence in the region. It provided unique insight on emerging business opportunities, enhanced our brand recognition in the youth market (college and university students) and opened business doors as few others have ever done in LAC. We envisioned a business plan competition for university students and required them to form interdisciplinary teams to present not only the technology but a complete business plan which included market studies, supply chain, R&D, legal and organizational issues. This was the first of such initiatives ever performed in LAC. Furthermore, it was launched simultaneously across the entire region and from its beginning was managed and fully administered using a centralized website that served the entire region.

A virtual team was assembled from the region and two recognized university professors were enlisted to provide the academic and logistical advice to penetrate the regional colleges and universities. The program was named Mission XXI (in Spanish) or Missâo XXI (in Portuguese). The Mission XXI business plan competition posters were proudly displayed at every university across the region and it captured the feelings and aspirations of the university students at the time. By the second quarter of 1998, Motorola launched Mission XXI promoting entrepreneurship and multidisciplinary teamwork, which empowered advanced university students to envision potential technology driven businesses demanded by the Latin American market.

Mission XXI became a tool, which provided over 500 businesses plans per year. While following a disciplined instrumental review development process, only several were worthy of executing. However, the entire set provided extraordinary information on market trends as well as insights and opportunities identified independently by students across the region.

Many other El Dorado Projects were developed, as was the norm, by small high power teams. Most of the projects dealt with different wireless technologies aiming to solve specific domain market opportunities. In doing so, timely information was made available concerning different assets such as vehicles, public utilities (i.e. electricity or gas) supply chain elements, etc. Seen in a philosophical light they all focused on a common issue in the region: wealth creation and loss. Inefficiency in the system often prevented the recirculation of wealth in the productive economy.

This approach gave El Dorado a unique competitive advantage which resulted from the businesses identified not being dependent on actual economic growth. All of the businesses were participating in already existing multi-billion dollar opportunity markets. The expected result was to obtain a value priced economic reward by making timely information available about their assets to owners, resource managers and other value chain stakeholders. The information would report about the in-transit objects to prevent what otherwise in the absence of these systems, would be misused, misplaced, misappropriate or 'disappear' from the productive circuit."

A Destiny Shared

P.Y. Lai (Chairman of Motorola in China) reviews the fundamental principles of building a partnership between a nation and a corporation, and what it takes to be successful. It also becomes apparent why a market entry in a high-class environment like China I so complex and rewarding at the same time.

Some of the programs and processes mentioned by P.Y. Lai have already been addressed in the previous chapters. They do, however, appear in a new light in the broad picture, which P.Y. Lai points out for us.

"Doing business in emerging markets is challenging but a great learning experience for those of us used to the culture of the market economy. For the market-based rule of law driven societies, rules are clearly defined and governance practices are transparent and predictable. The situation in the emerging market is somewhat different. It is best described by perhaps China's paramount leader Deng Xiao Peng, who had defined it as 'like feeling the stone underneath the water.' The environment is full of uncertainties that require the manager to react with flexibility, grounded on strong convictions that we are here to do good to the local community. In my 8 years operating in China, I have learnt to be guided by a win-win philosophy; i.e. bring benefits to the people and government in the market we are serving, at the same time taking care of the interest of the company and shareholders.

Companies enter a market to create value for its shareholders. At the same time we must bring real benefits to the people we are serving. In an emerging market like China, the regulatory infrastructure is not complete and policies governing foreign investment are evolving, which renders decision making very trying and uncertain. To do well it is important that we have the right mindset. From the beginning I have propounded a "Love and Sharing Philosophy" to the Motorola Board. By Love and Sharing we have to show our sincerity and patience, we need to demonstrate this in our tolerance of the evolving conditions in the country. In the Chinese culture to love means to share; sharing both the burden and the harvest. Hence our tolerance and patience to the market's imperfections and our constant participation and feedback to the authorities to make things better demonstrated our participation towards developing the local society and business.

Secondly, we ought to prove to our host nation that we are a friend of China. We do this through our many company policies and positions, for example Motorola's support of China's bid for the WTO. In times of crisis we should stand by our host nation and serve as a bridge to help resolve the tense situation/relations between our two nations.

Motorola went from a relatively small company of a few hundred million in revenue to a multi billion USD in China in less than a decade. She became China's largest foreign investor, China's most admired foreign employer, the foremost market leader in mobile phones. These results were brought about by our staunch commitment to developing Motorola into a Chinese company, respected by customers and employees alike.

Our success was guided by the following principles:

- Keep a keen eye on the policy of the country - policy environment and dynamics in the emerging market are always changing and evolving, hence we have to keep a close watch on the developments on the political front so that we can keep our corporate activities in line with the thinking of the day.

- Have a good grasp of local culture. Because the regulatory/legal environment is not developed, we have to rely on our cultural skills a lot. In China the economy was making a transition from a centrally planned economy to a market based one. Often the government plays a big role in the decision making of policies. Local and provincial leadership too have a large influence on decision making. This makes building and managing relationships a key skill to success. Three elements influence transactions: relationship, logic and legal elements. The reform in China began 20 years ago so many transactions are still governed by relationship. Managing strategic and critical relationships are fundamental to our China policy. In Motorola China, we spent a lot of time on our communication program with the leadership. We still make it a point to present our development plans and corporate focus for the year to the top central government leadership. We do this diligently so that key government leaders understand our development directions and are sure of our intentions and feel comfortable with our activities.

- Be involved with solving the problems of society. Uneven development and education are two challenges facing developing societies. In China, Motorola devoted a lot of resources in education, building HOPE schools (schools for the rural poor) and funding executive development programs for managers of the State Owned enterprise to help them cope better with the changing market place. To help bring development to the poorest areas Motorola was a pioneer in the Go-West initiative. We started to set up operations in the West (in Chengdu) long before the government started to promote investment in the West.

- Understand the political sensitivities between China and the United States of America. From the Bush Administration where the US was beginning to warm up to China to Bill Clinton's policy of looking upon China as a strategic partner, we constantly keep ourselves abreast of the latest thinking on Sino-US relations. Wherever there is an opportunity Motorola helps to contribute to further the development of constructive Sino-US relations.

Specifically in our approach in the China market our growth was guided by the following four-point strategy:

1. **Technology, Know-how and Investment for Market Share.** China needs technology, management know-how and investment to grow her industries. We are interested in her vast market. We position ourselves as a sincere partner who is genuine about their intention to develop China's industries; hence we are willing to transfer technology and know-how in exchange for China's opening of her market to our products.
2. **Localization of Management and Leadership.** Motorola launched extensive training programs and offered opportunities to the locals to fill important and key positions in the company. We make a concerted effort to localize our management and leadership. We systematically go about actualizing our pledge to turn Motorola China into a Chinese company.
3. **Localization in Content and Manufacturing.** We source local material and content four our products and outsourced production to local manufacturers creating jobs for thousands of local Chinese.
4. **Two Pronged Approach in Ownership/Operation Model.** We have wholly owned operations as well as joint ventures with locals. We try to be as inclusive as we can with local partners, sharing the fruits of development with them as well as jointly embarking on R&D efforts.

Motorola China's success can be attributed to our 'win-win' philosophy. Motorola's venture in China in the last eight years was rewarding for our employees and shareholders as well as for our Chinese partners and customers."

These two business cases underline the complexity of issues in major markets and what it takes to position ourselves as a local company. This is only possible by a strategy which links business with people. By enabling them to develop their skills and utilize their potential we gain access to untapped know-how, energy and motivation. With the tailwind of these assets we can achieve a much faster and better local integration.

Chapter 14 – The Price for Freedom and Prosperity

A Wake-Up Call

When Nelson Mandela left prison, he made a memorable statement: It was not him, but the whole country which was in prison. When we review the last hundred years, many countries were imprisoned. It was only with a unique effort involving much pain and many victims that they could liberate themselves. Never before have so many people regained their freedom and enjoyed a better life at once. In many countries, we face a quantum leap in terms of political stability, economic prosperity and social welfare.

History tells us that progress cannot be carried forward forever. It will be interrupted by phases of delays, stagnation or even destruction. Infrastructures, ecological systems and energy resources do not keep pace with growth, and counterproductive forces pursue a different agenda than ours. Some of the problems can only be resolved over time while others deserve our immediate attention.

The fast sequence of world events and their high unpredictability make us cautious about the medium-term future, a time span which we in business are still in the driver's seats of our companies and can influence their direction. I have therefore kindly asked Robert W. Galvin, Chairman Emeritus of Motorola Inc., to share with us his personal thoughts about some of the most burning issues, and what we can do about them.

"I happen to think that these are three transcending factors that will affect markets. I relate them particularly to the United States, but it doesn't take much imagination to see that the analog of what these matters are, vis-a-vis one country, will be ultimately an impacted factor in many, many other countries.

First, all markets are going to be affected within the next 10-20 years by the virtual belligerency of the Islamic movement. I deal with the issue without concern for political correctness. Islam is the great challenge of the world. The militant Islamists intend to set we infidels to the side, and they are going to disrupt markets all over the world, and we are going to have to stand up to them, those of us who wish to have a non-theocracy society. Whether the markets can emerge, or at least can expand as readily when the market place will be corrupted by this movement, is most unlikely.

Second, in the hopes that my belief expressed above does not mature to the severity that I'm afraid it will, there are two other issues that I believe are of transcending significance. First, this country, the United States, needs a robust energy system – that's slightly different than an energy policy which gets impacted by ecological subjects, concerns over cost controls at the regulation level, etc. I'm talking about the fact that a system has to be conceived instead of our having marginality as we now have, which is extremely costly to our society, and the system can fail with great frequency, sometimes for only a second or two to the immense cost to industry, and of course, every year or so, major failures like New York, the southern coast and most likely in many other countries.

I have taken on the personal responsibility of gathering together the brightest, boldest, most heretical thinkers to deal with this issue, and by next summer I hope to be publishing as a result of their scholarship and their creativity a very tangible, practical proposal as to how the electric system of the county should be radically changed, and that, of course, creates a market unto itself. It is when people determine that there is a big need for which resources are then applied, that new markets follow. I respectfully suggest that this will be something that will be affordable, every quality system is lower cost, and that we finally will have a system that will permit that our markets can perform without interruption from the standpoint of energy to drive the tools and the consumables of our society. That's a market elevator.

Third, if we do not solve the traffic congestion problem in the next 15-20 years, and absolutely have finished solving it by the middle of the century, almost all of the cities in the United States, and for that matter all around the world will die. Their vascular system, their traffic arteries, will stop functioning. The assets that have been put to work in the cities will be radically reduced in value, and in some instances, become valueless. If the body cannot function, the analog to our personal vascular system, then people will not be able to get to work, the work will not be serviceable, there will not be deliveries in equipments moved back and forth. There will not be the opportunity for commercial processes as well as human processes to be activated. I am convinced that the life of cities is now at complete risk.

So I am again gathering very bright scholars who are fascinated with the privilege to be able to think outside of all boxes, and come up with heretical ideas as to how to make it possible to move personal vehicles throughout major cities beginning early in the next decades, and absolutely by the middle of the half century, in a fashion that the assets that exist now and could be shortly added to our cities will retain their value because of the adequate convenience of delivery, transportation, personal travel interests, etc.

I am not applying any thoughts that represent any incrementalism. To me, these are severe absolutes, and if they are not dealt with in strong backbone leadership by those who should take cognizance of them, I do not hold out much hope for the conduct of markets after the middle of the century. In any country because all countries of any merit have big cities and big energy problems that they better solve assuming they can retain a governmental system no longer under the attack of we the infidels."

These statements about the energy and traffic problems remind us of the high and imminent vulnerability of the networks of modern civilization. As regards Islam, the expressed candid and independent opinion is a reflection of deep and widespread concerns. A sustained mobilization of the moderate religious forces of Islam could serve as a catalyst for intensifying the dialog on cultural diversity and mutual tolerance.

Although this wake-up call is of a global nature, it particularly affects the emerging markets because many of them are still in a fragile condition. It is vital that their accomplishments now and in the future are prevented from being endangered or even destroyed. Only together with these regions and countries as a new strong power will we be able to resolve the manifold issues ahead. After the memorable freedom movements and reform waves in the past 25 years, our society is now entering a new era. It will be our future obligation to preserve our values in face of a new dimension of uncertainties and to establish a workable balance between further uncontrollable growth, and the natural limitations of our global systems and resources. The two projects described above are an encouraging initiative. We need visionary leaders to prepare ourselves for the future.

> *Originally, emerging markets were just perceived as a source for incremental business. Throughout market entry we realised that their entire background must be taken into account as well. New markets can only be created on the basis of political and social stability, a functioning infrastructure, a high educational level, increasing wealth and compliance with the local conditions. By supporting the development of emerging countries and regions as a whole we do not only increase our opportunities but also strengthen the driving forces of the free world. Corporations which lay a lasting foundation in emerging markets with this understanding manifest global commitment.*

Appendix

A Business Plan

In Chapter 3 the importance of a business plan was described. It is therefore deemed appropriate to present such a plan, which summarizes the strategies, tactics and processes described. The reader is invited to use this plan or parts of it when planning an emerging market entry. The method applied is known as scenario planning.

1. Prioritize and Select Countries Based On

- Global/regional/country strategy of corporation
- Market assessment and potential
- Core competencies of the corporation
- Core competencies of the country
- Opportunities and barriers
- Internal and external driving forces

2. Determine Business Strategy

- Extent of local presence: total corporation or selected business units
- Offered portfolio of products and services
- Functions involved (Sales, Manufacturing, R&D etc)
- Local content needs and plans
- Highest internal and external effectiveness

3. Define Key Milestones

- Business goals
- Return on investment
- Major time frames subdivided into:
    Pre-startup
    Startup
    Consolidation
    Maintenance and expansion
- Requirement for resources, people and processes

- Speed and intensity required to achieve competitive edge
- Anticipation and early planning of possible change in direction as dictated by internal and external driving forces.
- Balanced allocation of investment and resources between the home country and other emerging markets
- A structured approach to ensure economies of scale
- A major concerted effort, a disciplined process and innovative ways
- Credibility in the market and our organization for what we do and how we do it

4. Identify the Critical Success Factors

- A dedicated resource in form of a high-level emerging market team will be provided headed by a champion to drive the market entry process
- The market entry needs to be approached in a unified manner. It would be ineffective, expensive and customer confusing to expect and allow our businesses to enter each country by themselves
- A due diligence test will be performed to establish an intelligent database for decision making
- The unified approach should allow for a sharing of the learning processes, resources, know-how and infrastructure and avoid all businesses going through the same learning and experience curves
- In appreciation of the many countries and markets, a stringent prioritization is necessary to ensure economies of scale and an optimal utilization of investment and resources
- An accelerated market entry has to ensure that the company stays ahead of competition and of market movement
- A Total Systems Approach needs to be applied to properly co-ordinate all activities and bundle all efforts
- Market entry has to be sub-divided into separate logical steps. They must be bold enough to support an aggressive market penetration, but also small enough to enable businesses to follow and change direction, if necessary
- The corporation needs to enhance market entry by a strategic budget to eliminate the natural limitations of the operational budgets
- The lack of adequate infrastructures and legislation requires up front investment into assisting and advising local governments in upgrading their countries. The organization must be prepared to go one step backwards, in order to create the framework for doing business
- Local presence is to be established to keep close to the market, show local commitment and build platforms for regional coverage and later expansion

- The corporation will invest into training and education to build a nucleus of a local workforce and to benefit from the untapped human resources
- The market entry strategy should emphasize added value programs that help overcome initial barriers, provide a competitive edge and enable a two-way transfer of knowledge to our mutual benefit
- Cooperations, alliances and joint ventures need to be formed to enlarge the operational platforms and to benefit from local know-how
- It is crucial to initiate programs that enhance the corporations' role as a technology leader, a good citizen and premier employer
- The market entry model should serve as a pattern for transfer of knowledge and know-how into other emerging markets.

Process Flow Chart

Emerging Market's Infrastructure Development
This tabulation covers those activities involved in setting up a local presence.

1.   Exploration and Start-Up Phase

1.1   Investigate information resources from

International regional organizations
Western and local ministries of economics
Embassies/consulates
Chambers of commerce
Western public accountants and their local affiliates
Western law firms and their local affiliates
Universities
Publication services
Internet/intranet
Recruitment agencies
Multinational companies
Corporate internal resources

**1.2   Gather available information and prepare initial country
report**

The report should include details on the country's:
History and culture
Demographics
Political system
Country infrastructure
Key economic indicators
Business climate
Opportunities and barriers
Legal framework
Types of company presence
Labor relations
Opportunities and risks
Migration trends
Competitive environment
Regulatory policy

1.3   Collect corporate and business plans and commitments from

Corporate Executive Office
Business General Management
Key Corporate Functions
Regional/Country Management

1.4   Conduct exploration visit to country and collect the following information

1.4.1   From a law firm:

Alternatives of local presence:
Representative office
Branch office
Subsidiary
Joint venture
Registration process (duration, cost)

Legal country framework:

The various law fields
Current legislation
Intellectual property rights
Jurisdiction
Legal structures and processes
Critical legislative issues
Employment terms and conditions:
Major employment terms
Probationary period
Termination of employment
Working hours
Vacation and holiday
Absenteeism
Overtime, etc.
Standard employment contracts
Temporary employment
Indefinite employment:
    Part-time employment
    Contract labor
    Consulting agreements
    Social security and health system
    Employer contribution

          Employee contribution
          Structure of schemes
          Work/residence permits

1.4.2   From public accountants:

Financial and accounting legislation that affect:
    Accounting system
    Accounts payable and receivable
    Payroll
    Cost accounting
    Financial accounting
    Profit and loss statements
    Closing dates
    Tax filing
    Statutory and compliance needs

Monetary policy:
Currency convertibility
Profit repatriation, etc.
Inflation rates

Employee compensation, including:
Income tax levels
Tax exemptions
Social security deductions
Payroll administration
Cost of living

Internal services, such as:
Accounting
Payroll
Financial services

1.4.3   From the embassy/consulate:

Government profile
Intelligence information /network
Pitfalls to be avoided
External aid money
Multinational companies in country
Memberships/associations
Living conditions for expatriates:
Housing

Schooling
Security

1.4.4   From the local government/chamber of commerce, learn about:

Country profile
Demographics
Government structure
Regulatory environment
Privatization
Structure of industry and commerce
Status and direction of economy
Country incentives

1.4.5   From the recruitment agency, determine:

Labor market
Skill levels and availability
Search practices and media
Salary levels
Managers
Professionals
Clerical
Salary review practices
Company benefits (pension, health, cars, etc.)
Search terms and conditions

1.4.6   From a local university, learn about the country's:

Educational system
Workforce profile
Skill strengths and weaknesses

1.4.7   From other multinational companies, learn about:

Their experiences
Compensation and benefit benchmarking
Networking

1.4.8   From a real estate agency, learn about:

Office availability
Lease and utility cost
Standard lease conditions

Local supplier availability for:
Furniture
Office equipment and machinery
Telecommunications
EDP

2.   Start-Up and Operations Phase

2.1   Found the company

2.1.1   Select appropriate legal form and carrier for accreditation and/or registration.

2.1.2   Provide and complete documents needed for accreditation and/or registration.

2.1.3   Identify company name and check appropriateness with local law firm.

2.1.4   Perform facility, security and environment audit of envisaged premises and prepare respective recommendation.

2.1.5   Identify and lease office.

2.1.6   Prepare and get approved office establishment documents

2.1.7   Prepare and appoint company legal representatives.

2.1.8   Select and identify local public accountants.

2.1.9   Establish petty-cash system for startup requirements.

2.1.10   Identify appropriate bank and open local bank account.

2.1.11   Provide banking authorizations.

2.1.12   Establish payroll and accounting system with local public accountants.

2.1.13   Provide proper legal layout for business cards and stationary.

2.2   Staffing and Employment

2.2.1   Obtain job descriptions and job grades for local corporate and business hires.

2.2.2   Determine local recruitment resources
Advertisements
Search firms
Universities

2.2.3   Prepare standard employment packages (salaries, benefits) and contracts.

2.2.4   Act as champion of corporate hires and assist businesses in their hiring activities.

2.2.5   Conclude employment contracts and ensure legal signature requirements.

2.2.6   Interface staffing and employment with local payroll.

2.2.7   Organize orientation program for new hires.

2.3   Facility Management

2.3.1   Prepare office layout in cooperation with local architect based on approved standard appropriation request (SAR).

2.3.2   Select appropriate suppliers and place orders for office furniture, security devices, equipment, machinery, telecommunications and EDP.

2.3.3   Physically supervise office facilitation preparation and furniture/equipment / machinery, telecom and EDP installation.

2.3.4   Provide bilingual signs and logos.

2.3.5   Coordinate process of premises occupation by local employees.

2.3.6   Prepare separate action plan for office opening.

3.   Organizational Integration

3.1   Ensure integration of local employees into office to share learning and resources and to increase synergy and corporate identity.

3.2   Assist regional management in institutionalizing country council, preparing Memorandum of Understanding and other management tools.

3.3   Provide local corporate support whenever critical mass is reached (human resources, finance, legal, government relations, facility management, etc.)

3.4   Play active role in managing the office and local operations in the country in compliance with key beliefs, goals and initiatives.

Country Information Gathering

The questions listed below are intended to be a guideline in the information gathering process and are, by far, not exhaustive.

Country Profile

1. What are the demographics of the country, how did they develop in the past and what are the expected future movements?

2. Which have been and are the main religious, cultural, social, ethnic, economic and political influence factors?

3. What is the historical, present and expected future relationship of the country with its neighbor states and within the geographic region?

4. Which significant lifestyle factors in terms of consumer behavior, cultural activities, sociability and home life can be observed?

5. How do the main economic indicators perform: GDP growth, capital expenditures, inflation, unemployment, etc.?

6. What are the key competencies of the country that might generate added value for companies like Motorola?

7. Who are the heroes that exist in the fields of politics, business, literature, music and other, and what is their impact on the population?

8. What legacy was left by the former political and economic systems, and to which extent does this still influence daily life?

9. Is the population rather introverted or extroverted, and what is the public opinion about current world trends?

10. What is the degree of literacy, which languages are spoken and what is the level of English proficiency?

11. How high is the crime rate and the general security standard?

Politics and Government

1. Which political system dominated in the past, is prevailing at present and is expected for the future?

2. What is the structure and power of the political parties in place?

3. Which parties is the government composed of (majority and minority composition)?

4. What is the structure of the present government and how strong or weak is it perceived?

5. Who are the key players, the winners and the losers in the present government?

6. Is the government stable or subject to frequent crisis and changes?

7. What is the government's policy and what are its generic priorities and needs?

8. What are the political alignments and influence spheres of the government?

9. To what extent is the government accepted and supported by the population?

10. Which role does the government play in the geographic context of the country and region?

Infrastructure

1. Is the country infrastructure well developed, of medium quality or still in a developing stage?

2. How is the infrastructure in the cities as compared to the countryside?

3. What is the quality of the road and transportation system in the cities and in the countryside, and how well is the country interconnected?

4. Which are the current traffic tariffs (air, water, railway, road)?

5. What is the quality and density of telephones, data lines and telecommunications services?

6. What is the availability and quality of hotels, restaurants and shops?

7. Which standards of medical care, hospitals and general health services can be observed?

8. Is the infrastructure conducive to our needs?

9. How much availability of adequate modern office space is there and what are the lease conditions?

10. What are the living circumstances for the expatriate community (housing, shopping, schooling, etc.)?

Regulatory Environment

1. Is the regulatory environment state-controlled, privatized and liberalized or in a transition stage?

2. To what extent does the government telecommunications policy and infrastructure correspond to the needs of the country?

3. Which government agencies and people handle telecommunications policy?

4. What are the procedures related to licensing, frequency management and type approvals?

5. Are the relevant regulations stand-alone or aligned to international standards and practices?

6. To what extent and under what conditions is private ownership possible?

7. Are there provisions for the protection of investment and intellectual property?

8. Do government and the responsible agencies and people promote or hinder regulatory issues?

Market Potential

1. What is the market potential for our individual sectors, groups and divisions in which market segments?

2. How do the company's core competencies and portfolio match with this potential?

3. How are these market segments structured and developed, and who are the key players?

4. To what extent are these markets accessible or closed?

5. Which strategies and processes should be applied to ensure a smooth and efficient market penetration?

6. Are there markets that may support the development of new, or modifications of existing products?

7. What is the profile of our potential customers, distributors, suppliers, and other partners?

8. Which of Motorola businesses are already directly or indirectly present in which markets, and to what extent?

9. How can the businesses benefit from the already existing contacts and networks?

10. What is the history of our existing customers and distributors?

11. Which other cooperations and alliances exist in the marketplace on which the company can further expand?

Business Climate

1. What are the opportunities and barriers in the country for a company?

2. Is the government inviting foreign companies and investment on the grounds of attractive conditions?

3. What is the general attitude toward, and perception of, foreign companies and nationals among the government and population?

4. Are there economic and financial aid programs particularly designed and available for the country?

5. In what international economic and business organizations does the country have a membership?

6. Are there substantial efforts to improve the general business climate or is the attitude rather passive?

7. What ethics and other value systems determine the business practices?

Trade Terms and Conditions

1. Is property acquisition allowed and, if yes, when?

2. Are there limitations on majority ownership in local businesses such as joint ventures?

3. Are there relevant US sanctions or embargoes affecting business activities?

4. Are there boycott measures of the country excluding or limiting business activities?

5. Which types of products or business must the company access through a distributor?

6. Is profit expatriation legally allowed?

7. Is there a requirement for local content such as manufacturing?

8. What are the regulations for barter and countertrade?

9. What are the current import/export customs procedural tariffs?

10. Which rules pertain to local licensing agreements?

11. Are there technical barriers to trade (e.g. type approvals)?

Competition

1. Which competitors are present in which market segment?

2. What are the competitors' profiles regarding strategies, processes, technology, alliances, market share, logistics, government relations, image, management, workforce, etc.?

3. Are there competitors that are customers at the same time?

4. Are there benefits of cooperation and partnering in areas without potential conflicts of interest?

5. Do we possess intelligence information about the competitors that may help our assessment?

Management Style

1. How could we describe the overall management style: conservative, progressive, self-sufficient, liberal?

2. To what extent is the management style still influenced by the old school?

3. Is the attitude toward new ideas and change positive, neutral or negative?

4. What are the accepted customs and norms?

5. How high is the availability of Western management theory and practice? Can it be trained?

6. What are the work ethic and performance standards?

7. Is there evidence of participative behavior?

8. How is the relationship between management and the workforce?

9. How is current management perceived in the public opinion?

Labor Relations

1. What is the labor relations structure of the country?

2. Within which frameworks are employers' associations and unions working together?

3. Which types of collective agreements are applicable to foreign companies?

4. What structure of internal employee representation exists with what responsibilities?

5. What are the rights and strategies of the unions?

6. Are companies unionized or can they stay union-free?

7. What is the unionization grade in the country and in companies?

8. Under which circumstances can strikes take place and what are the average strike rates?

9. How is the general labor relations climate?

10. What are the most critical labor relations issues?

Employment

1. What are the governing labor and employment laws in the country?

2. What is the source of current labor legislation? Is it country-focused or based on Western models?

3. Which typical employment categories are there in a company: exempt, non-exempt, salaried employees, wage earners, permanent and temporary employees?

4. What types of employment contracts exist?

5. Are we able to test potential employees, and are background checks allowed?

6. Are there equal employment opportunity laws or other minority protection regulations?

7. What are the provisions for collective or individual dismissal and legal termination?

8. What are the procedures for major layoffs and redundancy payments?

9. Which laws govern relevant safety, health and environment?

10. How is the ruling of labor courts: in favor of employer or employee, or strictly neutral?

11. What are the local and national compensation levels for benchmark jobs?

12. What evidence is their of compensation data for benchmark jobs?

13. What are the current employment terms?

- Working hours
- Vacation and holidays
- Probationary and termination policies
- Overtime and shift regulations
- Social security scheme
- Legal and company fringe benefits
- Salary and inflation adjustments
- Employer and employee contributions

Human Resources

1. What is the structure and quality of the public educational system?

2. What is the general educational standard?

3. How is the demographic distribution of education: higher, medium, lower levels?

4. Which critical skills are to be found in the region and country?

5. What search mechanism is in place in the labor market: advertising, university contacts, direct search, word of mouth, etc.?

6. What is the trainability, adaptability and employability of the workforce?

7. Which intellectual capabilities are of interest as a potential labor resource for the Western world?

8. How well is the human resource function recognized and established in the country?

Communications/Public Relations

1. What is the structure and position of the classical media in the country: TV, radio, newspapers, journals, etc.?

2. Is the communications policy of the government liberal or restricted?

3. Are the media playing a strong political role in the country and, if yes, in which direction?

4. What advertising and public relations institutions are in place?

5. How can we use the media to generate brand awareness in the country?

6. What is the attitude of the media toward foreign companies?

7. Are there modern communication tools and facilities in place?

Legal/Intellectual Property Rights

1. How is legislation structured and what is the historical and cultural background?

2. Is current legislation more conservative or progressive, protective or liberal?

3. Is legislation generally ahead or behind macro-changes in the country?

4. To what extent was legislation adjusted to Western role models?

5. Is legislation stable or subject to frequent changes?

6. Is jurisdiction fair or in favor or disfavor of certain parties?

7. Are intellectual property rights adequately protected or are copyrights, patents and trademarks at risk?

8. What are the provisions against trademark piracy, blackmail, counterfeit goods and gray markets?

9. What types of legal company presence exist for which business activities?

10. Are there potential conflict areas pertaining to the company's code of conduct?

11. What are the legislation fields most critical to the company?

Finance

1. Are finance and accounting laws and regulations meeting the requirements of current economy and business state?

2. Is legislation generally ahead or behind macro-changes in the country?

3. Are laws unequivocal or do they leave room for unwanted interpretation?

4. Are there potential conflicts of interest with the company's standards of internal control?

5. What is the local tax structure (corporate, value added, income taxes, key holdings etc)?

6. Does current tax legislation allow us to meet our business and profit goals?

7. Are authorities aware of and responsive to the business needs of Western corporations?

8. What are the most critical finance, accounting and tax issues impacting our way of doing business?

Manufacturing/ Engineering/ R&D

1. Is there appropriate land for a new construction that may be acquired or leased?

2. Are there adequate buildings/facilities, which may be acquired or leased?

3. Are there possibilities for a condominium factory?

4. What are the terms and conditions for option 1 to 3?

5. Is the local environment suitable for our type of operation?

6. Does the local infrastructure match our needs?

7. Is there a functioning supply chain management guaranteed?

8. Can we obtain Western or local grants/incentives for our investment?

9. Does the quality and layout of the envisaged building/facility meet our standards?

10. Are there enough process flexibility and/or modification/expansion possibilities in the planned building/facility?

11. What are the potential liabilities in the existing building/facility or condominium operation?

12. Can we take over available machinery/equipment?

13. What are the regulations and cycle times for importing/exporting machinery/equipment, materials and finished products?

14. Are there qualified suppliers and/or subcontractors available? If not, what are the qualification requirements?

15. What are the forecasted utility, overhead and operating costs?

16. Is there a functioning effluent water/waste disposal system?

17. Can raw/semi-finished material be processed locally?

18. Is there a reliable energy supply?

19. Are there critical skills available in the local labor market?

20. Do the safety and security standards meet our standards?

Regional Aid Programs

The organizations and institutions listed below grant financial aid and provide support and service in the fields of regional economic infrastructure, social and educational development:

1. **Global Coverage**

    Inter American Development Bank (IDB), Washington D.C.

    International Bank for Reconstruction and Development (IBRD), Washington D.C.

    International Finance Corporation (IFC), Washington D.C.

    International Investment Guarantee Agency (MIGA), Washington D.C.

    International Monetary Fund (IMF), Washington D.C.

    United Nations Development Program (UNDP), New York

    Overseas Private Investment Corporation (OPIC), Washington D.C.

2. **Africa**

    African Development Bank (ADB) in association with the African Development Fund (ADF), Abidjan, Ivory Coast

    Africa, Caribbean and Pacific Program of European Investment Bank (ACP), London

    Arab Bank for Economic Development in Africa (ABFDA), Chartenis

    Export Development Bank of Egypt (EDBC), Cairo

    Development Program of the United Nations for the African Region (UNDP), New York, in association with:

    - Enterprise Africa Program
    - Private Sector Promotion Center
    - African Management Service Company

    United Nations Economic Commission for Africa (ECA), Addis Adeba

    New Partnership for African Development (NEPAD), Johannesburg

3. **Asia**

Asian Development Bank (ADB), Manila

Asian Investment Program of European Union, Brussels

China Council for the Promotion of International Trade (CPIT) in association with China Chamber of Industrial Commerce (CCOIC), Beijing

India Trade Promotion Organization (PIT), New Delhi

Philippine Trade Investment Promotion Office (PTIP), Manila

Malaysian International Development Authority (MIDA), Koala Lumpur

Thailand Bank of Investment (TBOI), Bangkok

4. **Central and Eastern Europe**

European Bank for Reconstruction and Development (EBRD), London

European Investment Bank (EIB), London

European Union (EU), Brussels:

(TACIS) Technical Assistance Program for Commonwealth of Independent States

(ENI) European Neighbour Instrument (effective 2007)

Structural and Cohesion Funds (structural implementation)

(SAPARD) Special Accession Program for Agricultural and Rural Development

(CARDS) Community Assistance for Reconstruction, Development and Stabilization of Balkan Countries

(MEDA) Assistance Program for Mediteranean Belt States

5. **Latin America**

Agencia de Desarrollo de Inversiones (ADI), Buenos Aires

AL Investment Program of European Union, Brussels

Corporacion Andina de Fomento (CAF), Caracas

European Development Fund for Latin America (EEF), European Union

Indo-American Development Bank (IDB), New York (regional offices in all countries)

Investment Promotion and Technology Transfer (SIPRI), Brasilia

Mexico Bank for Foreign Trade (Barcomext), Mexico City

Pro Chile, Santiago de Chile

6. **The Middle East**

Abu Dhabi Chamber of Commerce and Industry (ADCCI), Abu Dhabi, UAE

Bahrain Chamber of Commerce and Industry, Mamana

Commerce and Tourism Promotion Board, Dubai

Investment Promotion Corporation Amman, Jordania

Investment and Development Authority of Lebanon (DAC), Beirut

Kuwait Investment Authority, Safar

MEDA-Program of European Union, Brussels

Quatar Chamber of Commerce and Industry, Doha

Saudia Arabian General Investment Authority (SAGIA), Riad

Saudi Industrial Development Fund (SIDF), Riad

The United Center for Investment Promotion and Export Development (OCIPED), Oman

Regional Organizations and Institutions

The following organizations and institutions:

- Promote regional political stability, economic growth and social welfare
- Enhance bilateral, regional and global co-operation and integration, improve investment climate and free trade conditions
- Render special support and services

1. Africa

Common Market for Eastern and Southern Africa (Comesa), Lusaka

Common Market for Sahel Saharan States (Comessa), Tripoli

Economic Community of West African States (ECOWAS), Lagos

Economic and Monetary Unit of Central Africa (CEMAC), Bangui, Central Africa

Southern Africa Development Community (SADC), Cabone

African Union (AU), Addis Abeba (formerly OAU, Organization for African Unity)

The Commonwealth of Nations, London

2. Asia

Asia-Pacific Economic Co-operation (APEC), Singapore

Association of South East Asian Nations (ASEAN), Jakarta

Economic and Social Commission for Asia and the Pacific (ESCAP), Bangkok

South Asian Association for Regional Cooperation (SAARC), Kathmandu

3. Central and Eastern Europe

Central European Free Trade Agreement (CEFTA), Rotating, see www.cefta.org

Commonwealth of Independent States (CIS), Minsk

Council of the Baltic States, Stockholm

European Free Trade Association (EFTA), Geneva

European Union (EU), Brussels

Organization for Economic Co-operation and Development (OECD), Paris

Organization for Safety and Cooperation in Europe, (OSZE), Vienna

4. **Latin America**

Caribbean Community and Common Market (CARICOM), Greater Georgetown, Guyana

Free Trade Area of the Americas (FTAA), Rotating,
see www.ftaa-alca.org

Community of Andean Nations (CAN), Lima

North American Free Trade Association (NAFTA), Washington D.C.

Organization of American States (OAS), Washington D.C.

South American Common Market (Mercosur) Montevideo

5. **The Middle East**

League of Arab States, Cairo

Organization of Petroleum Exporting Countries (OPEC), Vienna

Gulf Cooperation Council (GCC), Riad

Organization of the Islamic Conference, Dschidda

About Motorola

Founded in 1928 in Chicago as the Galvin Manufacturing Corporation, the young company had to forge its way through the critical years of world recession. The first product, a battery eliminator, was followed by a broad range of technological breakthroughs; the two-way radio in its basic, hand held and transistorized versions, the power transistor, the space communicator, the cellular phone, the 8 bit micro processor and data communications to name only a few. A Motorola receiver was part of the communications equipment to be found on the first lunar vehicle.

In the past 50 years Motorola has changed its position from a domestic company with export business to a multinational corporation with local presence in all world regions. Today, Motorola is a global leader in wireless communications, integrated electronic applications and many other advanced technologies for the public and private sectors. The large portfolio of products, systems and tailored customer solutions serve the end user at home, at work and on the move. The business volume in the emerging markets as defined in this book grows steadily and over-proportionally compared to Motorola's overall performance.

In 2004 Motorola completed the separation of its semiconductor business into an independent company called Freescale Semiconductor, Inc.

Since Motorola's foundation, three generations of the Galvin family have stood for an outstanding role model of American pioneering, which is geared to continue under new leadership.

(I have refrained from reporting any sales, employment and other key numbers since they tend to date quickly. For these details and further information about Motorola, please refer to www.motorola.com)

About the Author

Guenter Schoenborn joined Motorola in 1978 as Director of Human Resources for Germany and was subsequently appointed as Director of Human Resources for the European Radio Communications business.

In 1990, he accepted the challenge of becoming Director of Human Resources for Emerging Markets, comprising Central and Eastern Europe and expanded to the Middle East and Africa in 1993. His responsibilities included the development of the organizational and human resources infrastructure in these regions. He led the process of setting up more than 15 local offices and subsidiaries. He was also extensively engaged in a range of global emerging market assignments.

Prior to joining Motorola, Guenter Schoenborn was Personnel Director and Manager of Training and Education in various multinational companies located in Germany.

Guenter Schoenborn received a master's degree in Business Administration in 1961 and has done extensive lecturing and writing throughout his career. After his retirement in 1996, he started consulting work with emphasis on emerging markets and labor relations. He lives with his family near Wiesbaden in Germany.

From July 1999 to May 2004, Guenter Schoenborn was Chairman of the Supervisory Board of Motorola, Germany. He received the President's Award from Motorola University for writing the first version of the book.

Printing and Binding: Strauss GmbH, Mörlenbach